AGAINST THE GRAIN

AGAINST the GRAIN

Ditch the American Dream and Create Your Own!

CRAIG A. PERKINS

LIONCREST
PUBLISHING

AGAINST THE GRAIN
Ditch the American Dream and Create Your Own!

ISBN 978-1-5445-2542-6 *Hardcover*
    978-1-5445-2541-9 *Paperback*
    978-1-5445-2543-3 *Ebook*

To my beautiful daughter, Brenna.

May you use this book as your compass when you
find yourself lost on the Path called Life.

Success equals autonomy.

ENDURE!

CONTENTS

INTRODUCTION

WE'VE ALL BEEN LIED TO!

"Whatever paths you chose, someone will hate you. Only be certain that someone is not you!"

—S.D. SIMPER

Get good grades in high school. Pick a profession based on high income and social status, and go to the most prestigious college that will accept you. Land a Fortune 500 job and claw your way up the corporate ladder. Get used to driving in nine-to-five traffic every day. Marry your sweetheart and purchase a home with debt. Have children and start saving for their college educations the day after they are born. Relish your three to four weeks of vacation each year. Retire after working for 40 years building someone else's business. Enjoy the last 15 years of your life.

Who, in their right mind, would willingly sign up for this life? It sounds more like a prison sentence than the best-case scenario of a life well lived. I can't remember a time

I heard a high school senior say, "I can't wait to graduate from college and drive in traffic every day for the pleasure of sitting in a cubicle where I'll spend most of my time daydreaming about doing something exciting on the weekend." Is this what each of us expected life to be like when we were young? When we rode our bikes, climbed trees, and had fun with our friends? We all know the answer to that question is a resounding *no*!

So why do most of us follow this Path in life? The answer is simple: Society lied to us and told us it was the only way. Our parents and teachers, who also believed the lie, taught us the same thing.

Society needs us to think this way to keep the supply chain full of brainwashed employees, willing to trade fulfillment for Corporate America's need for ever-growing profits. Let me be the first to admit *I took the bait—hook, line, and sinker.*

If you're reading this book, I bet you've also believed the lie. Now, you've boxed yourself into a life that provides comfort but very little authenticity.

You're stressed and working an unfulfilling job. You have a big mortgage, small savings, and a couple of leased cars in the garage. You've got lots of toys and gadgets to keep you occupied on the weekends, and some addiction to drugs or alcohol to help you cope with the emptiness of it all.

You've achieved the American Dream! Your life is considered normal in America. Your college education and hard work have finally paid off. But you end every weekend with the Sunday Scaries, that dull feeling of dread lingering in your head as you look ahead to the next five days. As you set the alarm on your cell phone, you listen to that voice from deep within that asks the same old question, "Is this all there is to life?" You lay your head down on your pillow and think: "There has to be a better way!" You are desperate to make a fundamental change in your life, but you don't know how to get started. Hell, you probably don't even know what else you would do.

That's okay. I wrote this book for you. I wrote it to show you how to plot an alternate route to Society's Path, with instructions for breaking out of Society's Box. This is the box most of us put ourselves in around the time we have to answer that shitty little question, "What are you going to do when you grow up?"

Who the hell knows what they want to do with their life when they are 18 years old? We don't, so we do what everyone else is doing. We take the easy Path and listen to Society's lies. What I've learned firsthand is that spending your life trying to fit into Society's Box of "the way you are supposed to be" is a sure way to lose.

Society's Path has its compass set on a final destination

best described as "He who dies with the most toys wins." Those who seek to keep you in Society's Box understand the only way to lessen the dread of your day-to-day existence is the jolt of dopamine produced by your next big purchase. It's a sinister system designed by Society, leading to never-ending consumer spending and fatter and fatter corporate bank accounts. Trying to justify living a life bereft of any real Purpose by pointing to all the "things" you own is like lying to yourself about how healthy you are with an LDL cholesterol level exceeding 300 mg/dl. It's a big fat lie.

I watched two essential men in my life take very different paths. My father died angry at the world after chasing wealth and status throughout his life. My maternal grandfather died a happy and fulfilled man without ever living in anything nicer than a single-wide trailer. One followed Society's Path with the rest of the herd. The other followed his own Path and didn't concern himself with the opinions of others. I should have listened to my grandfather when I was young. Instead, I listened to my father. I took my father's advice and graduated from college with a bachelor's degree in mechanical engineering and landed an excellent job with a Fortune 500 company. I climbed the corporate ladder quickly, becoming the youngest plant manager in the company's history.

To the outside world, I was a complete success. I was in my early thirties, recently married, and a new homeowner. I was in charge of a manufacturing plant that employed over 500 employees and sold over $50 million worth of bearings to United States automakers. I made a six-figure income with stock options that was vested every five years I stayed with the company.

But the truth was bottled up inside of me. I never wanted to be an engineer. I wanted to be a football coach. I only selected engineering as my major in college because it was my father's dream. The dream of a man who grew up on a farm with a brother and two sisters, required to share the same tub of hot water to take their nightly baths. A father who had gone to the same high school I attended, but went in each morning smelling like barnyard animals after doing his early morning chores. A father who lived his entire life trying to prove to the world he wasn't that poor kid they remembered back within the halls of Putnam High.

More than anything, my father wanted my brother and me to get good white-collar jobs and not struggle as he had throughout his life. To him, that meant a college education and a status-filled corporate position. I listened to my father and started making him proud. I'll never forget the times I went back home and had breakfast with my father and his friends. In the middle of breakfast, he would announce that I had recently received another promotion. He'd look at me and ask, "Craig, how much money are you making now?" Little did he realize, each promotion only got me further away from what I enjoyed doing, and a little more filled with the "embalming fluid" of Corporate America, a term perfectly coined by Hap Klopp, founder of The North Face, in his outstanding book *The Adventure of Leadership: An Unorthodox Business Guide.*

Every time I looked into a mirror, I found myself asking the guy looking back at me, "What the hell are you doing with your life?" From what I could tell, Corporate America filled itself with midlevel managers who were the smart kids in high school—the ones who were picked on and bullied. Those same high school kids now had impressive titles on their business cards and enjoyed bullying their subordinates. It was payback in some way. The higher I climbed the corporate ladder, the more ass-kissing and lying came from my superiors. The culture of upper management disgusted me. There was simply no way I was staying in this Box for the next 30 years. I was drowning in the embalming fluid of Corporate America.

For me, there was only one way to survive. Against the advice of everyone around me, I quit my job as plant manager. I started a consulting business with the division's chief cost accountant. I had always wanted to be my own boss, and this was the quickest, least costly way of dipping my toe into that pond. Everyone around me told me I was crazy for quitting such a great job. My father didn't want to talk to me, and I lost many of the "friends" I thought I had at my corporate job. It was a difficult time. Little did I know, I had stumbled onto a very different Path. A Path with a barely visible trailhead sign that read "Against the Grain."

> *Against the grain (idiom): Contrary to what is expected; especially, of behavior different from what society expects (Wiktionary.org).*

The Path was overgrown with brush and fallen trees from lack of use. It was so steep in certain places that fear of failure stopped most people in their tracks. The Path was so long and lonely, it would have been easy to give up and follow one of the many well-groomed trails back to the trailhead. Trails aptly called "Parents' Advice," "Friends' Warnings," "Management Bonuses and Stock Options," and "Keeping Up with the Joneses."

Whenever I veered down one of the well-groomed trails, a voice deep inside started whispering in my ear, "You're headed in the wrong direction, Craig." In the beginning, I often wondered who was behind that voice. I've learned over the past 20 years that the voice holding me accountable was, in fact, my Authentic Self. It's a voice within each of us. Most of us stop listening to that voice by the time we reach middle school, and instead we start listening to everyone else's. The single most important lesson I have learned in life is this:

Success in life requires listening closely to your Authentic Self.

You must listen to your Authentic Self *before* you start down this much more difficult Path. Failure to listen to your Authentic Self will always result in ending up right back where you started.

Little did I know when I first quit my job in Corporate America, I had gone from living a life planned and orchestrated by others' expectations to suddenly having the opportunity to create a life filled with Freedom. The Freedom to always drive in the opposite direction of traffic. The journey has been challenging and equally exciting. It has *never* been boring.

The consulting business led to the purchase of a failing World Gym. I also became one of Planet Fitness's first franchisees, joined a partnership in an indoor trampoline park startup, and eventually partnered with my wife as a Sola Salon Studio franchisee.

Going Against the Grain is a daunting endeavor. Breaking away from the herd requires self-confidence and an obsession with staying true to yourself. If you commit to the plan and refuse to give up, your life will become like the picture on this book's cover. You'll create a life where you are always driving in the opposite direction of traffic. A life filled with personal Freedom.

Think of the autonomy of not having to be at work at a specific time each day, adhering to some acceptable dress code, and hoping for your 3 to 4 percent annual increase from a boss you don't even respect. You can create a life with the Freedom to go to Costco at 10:00 a.m. on a weekday when the checkout lines are empty, or meet your spouse at 3:00 p.m. on a Tuesday to start happy hour. You can create the Freedom to spend three months in Florida and help your mother recover from a traumatic brain injury. You can have the Freedom to volunteer at your daughter's school and be a regular chaperone on her class trips, soliciting funny looks from the mothers of her classmates (if you're a dad), and answering the commonly asked question, "What do you do for a living?"

The foundation of my Freedom has been owning a business with robust operating systems, and having committed and well-trained employees who think and act like owners. When you own your own business and do something that connects with you on an emotional level every day, you can create your own world. A world with a "work" community of employees who believe in your company's Vision, and a "play" community of friends and family who share your passions. It's a life full of autonomy, and it's obtainable. I know, because I live this life.

My "work" was helping gym members improve their health and fitness. My "play" was racing motocross and go-karts. I got to schedule my calendar with what I wanted to do, not what someone in the corner office wanted me to do. Today, my weeks revolve around helping coach my daughter's soccer, basketball, and lacrosse teams, caring for my mother as she struggles with dementia, and supporting my wife as Sola Salon franchisees.

I am not the founder of a wildly successful company. I am not a professional athlete or a Medal of Honor recipient. I am just a smaller-than-average guy from a smaller-than-average New England town, who learned the value of hard work at a young age from a demanding father. I learned to believe in myself and had the confidence to overcome the obstacles in my life. I learned from excellent coaches the value of teamwork to reach any goal. I began my life playing by Society's rules, but I will end it playing by my own. It's a crazy good life, and one I believe everyone should strive to create.

Use this book as a guide to create an autonomous life. Use it to plan your escape from Society's Box. Use it to get ready, both physically and mentally, before attempting such a rigorous expedition. I had no idea what I was doing when I took the Path called Against the Grain. Much of what I did was reactionary, many times based purely on emotion. I came close to turning around more times than I care to admit. I was lucky to have survived. What saved me time and time again was that little voice whispering in my ear,

"You can do better than this. You've never been someone to follow the herd. Stop trying to fit in!"

If you're looking for more autonomy in your life, I wrote this book for *you*. But it comes with a "warning" taped to the outside cover:

"If your goal in life is to be the next Jeff Bezos, with a private jet and multimillion- dollar homes filled with exotic cars, this book is NOT for you."

My very wealthy friends have allowed me to drive Ferraris, fly in private jets to watch Super Bowl games and UFC events, and enjoy meals cooked by personal chefs in 18,000-square-foot homes. I am beyond thankful, and it's all been wicked fun. But that wasn't my Path toward authentic Freedom. Make sure your desire for wealth doesn't rob you of your Freedom. I know too many individuals and families who have become prisoners to their own success.

I've seen firsthand what a high level of entrepreneurial success can create. More chains. Less Freedom. A work life so demanding it overwhelms your personal life, and eventually prevents you from doing activities outside of work you have always loved. You must know when to say "enough" before you even start down this Path to greater autonomy. Once you establish what it would take to make you feel free and you reach it, stop and enjoy the autonomy you've created. Don't make the mistake of continually trying to raise the bar.

Please don't wake up someday and realize you can't even find peace within the walls of your own home. Don't get to the point where you have to look at a schedule to see when your house will be empty so you won't run into the person cleaning it, cooking in it, repairing it, or maintaining the grounds. Don't allow yourself to become so successful you have to change the phone number you've had your entire life because you keep getting calls from old friends looking to borrow a little money. What's wrong with them asking to borrow $100,000 when they know you are worth $100 million?

That doesn't sound like Freedom to me.

This book, at its essence, is about going Against the Grain. It's about jumping off Society's Path and breaking out of Society's Box. It's about living the life *you* want to live, not the one Society or anyone else thinks you should be living. Going Against the Grain is about living your Authentic Life. Mine is rooted in autonomy. I'm always looking to call my own shots and live each day on my terms.

We all have this potential life in front of us, but we seldom even notice it. We embrace Society's lies and our own ego's never-ending need for self-gratification. We walk right by the door that opens to our Authentic Life, day after day after day. On the days when following Society's Path crushes our soul, we may finally see the door and even try to turn the handle. But it's always locked. Opening the door to your Authentic Life is never that easy.

Throughout the initial chapters, I will give you instructions to build a small, three-legged step stool. You know, the kind of stool you typically see stuck in the far corner of some closet. The one people use to reach the stuff stored on the shelf above the clothes that hang below. It's the stool you need to reach the key hidden on the molding above that door to your Authentic Life. Without the step stool, you'll never open the door. It will stay locked forever. But if you do the work explained in the early chapters, you'll build the stool needed to reach the hidden key. In the later chapters, you'll learn the Guiding Principles required to succeed on the Path called Against the Grain and live an Authentic Life.

This book is for the high school student still struggling to figure out what she wants to do when she grows up. It's for the college student who realizes the major he picked is no longer enjoyable. It's for the new employee drowning in the embalming fluid of Corporate America, wondering how she ever selected this career in the first place.

The earlier in life you read this book, the better. The

younger you start on the Path called Against the Grain, the easier the climb will be. This book is written for anyone with the confidence and drive to stop following the herd on Society's Path and become their own boss. It's for the person who doesn't care about status and trying to impress everyone—the person who is okay with living in a modest home, driving an older car, and creating the time to immerse himself in memorable experiences. It's for the person who wants to be available for a weekday round of morning golf, an early afternoon workout at the gym, or a weekday hike in the mountains. It's for the person who wants to live a life filled with autonomy. A life lived on their own terms.

If your goal is personal Freedom, the Path will be Against the Grain. When done correctly, following your Purpose will result in a life filled with autonomy. We'll discuss Purpose later in the book, but the picture on the front cover of this book says it all for me. For the last 25 years, I've had the Freedom to drive in the opposite direction of traffic. I only go shopping when there are no lines. I go to the movies when I can pick any seat in the house. I immerse myself in activities I am obsessed with. I have time to help care for my family when they need me most. Life is so much more enjoyable when you live it on your terms and focus on what matters to you and the ones you love. My real hope is that my daughter, Brenna, learns from this story that she can do the same.

Please read on if you are ready to break out of Society's Box and follow a more rewarding Path in life. It all begins by figuring out what Freedom means to *you*. Don't wait, stop worrying, and start now!

CHAPTER 1

—

WHO ARE YOU LISTENING TO?

"When you truly don't care what anyone thinks of you, you have reached a dangerous level of freedom."

—JIM CARREY

"Craig, have you lost your mind?" My father's voice was full of irritation. "You want to quit your plant manager job and start your own business? You are only 32 years old, and already make more money in a year than I ever have. You are going to regret this decision. If you do something stupid like this, don't come running to me if things don't work out. You are an engineer with an MBA and a plant manager with a great company. This decision just doesn't make any sense. I know you don't like your new boss, but keep your head down and do your job. You have too much to lose. What the hell does your wife have to say about this?"

It's so damn hard to go Against the Grain and live authentically. The minute you speak words about doing something outside Society's norms and listen to that little voice in your heart that understands what gives you goose bumps, the naysayers come out of the woodwork. Parents and close friends are either too risk-averse, or they don't want to see someone in their circle break free and succeed. How dare you try and do something that may make them look foolish for plodding along with the rest of the herd on the long road to retirement and a house near the beach in Florida?

You must become deaf to the naysayers, or you'll never break away from the herd.

Go ahead and tattoo that on your forearm so you see it every day. Read the famous section "The Man in the Arena," from Teddy Roosevelt's speech "Citizenship in a Republic." I want you to *feel* the words:

It is not the critic who counts; not the man who points out how the strong man stumbles, or where the doer of deeds could have done them better. The credit belongs to the man who is actually in the arena, whose face is marred by dust and sweat and blood; who strives valiantly; who errs, who comes short again and again, because there is no effort without error and short-coming; but who does actually strive to do the deeds; who knows great enthusiasms, the great devotions; who spends himself in a worthy cause; who at the best knows in the end the triumph of high achievement, and who at the worst, if he fails, at least fails while daring greatly, so that his place shall never be with those cold and timid souls who neither know victory nor defeat.

To go Against the Grain and follow your Purpose, you need to become deaf to the critics, including the toughest one that lives inside your head. Tim Urban so expertly labels this inner voice our "Social Survival Mammoth." The process of finding Personal Freedom begins with reexamining your Authentic Self and gaining the confidence to start listening to that voice. The voice originating from your heart knows who you are, and what brings happiness and joy to your life.

I grew up with parents who were controlled by their Mammoth minds. My father grew up poor on a farm and did everything he could in life to overcome the perception of how he believed others judged him. He was obsessed with purchasing material things to show others how successful he had become. My mother grew up in the era of subservient wives, obliged by some Neanderthal concept that a husband should have total control over each person in their nuclear family. My parents only had high school educations and firmly believed their children needed to attend college to live better lives. They were determined to give my brother and me everything they didn't have growing up.

My childhood was a combination of working my ass off with my brother and father, building our "plantation," and playing on our 63 wooded acres with dirt bikes, snowmobiles, and guns whenever we had free time. But my true love centered around team sports and competition. As I grew older and needed to figure out what I wanted to do when I grew up, my father always gave me a clear and concise answer: "You want to be an engineer like my friend, Eric."

Eric owned his own construction company and lived in a 12,000-square-foot home in a nearby town. He was one of the wealthiest men in northeast Connecticut. I always brushed off the idea because I learned you needed to excel in math to become an engineer. I did okay in math, but it certainly wasn't a class I looked forward to attending. The closer I got to high school graduation, the more my father talked about me going to college to become an engineer.

When it came time to start applying to colleges, a series of events occurred that explained how listening to the wrong people keeps so many of us from finding our Authentic Selves. I loved everything about my high school years, both in the classroom and on the athletic playing fields. I ended up ranking twelfth academically in my graduating class, was a member of the National Honor Society, co-captain of my football team, and an all-state honorable mention running back. I worked hard, studied hard, and played hard. But like an annoying parrot perched on my shoulder, my father never stopped squawking that I needed to be an engineer if I wanted to be wealthy and successful. He had no idea that all I wanted to be was a high school gym teacher and head football coach.

No one had a more positive influence on my life during my high school years than my head football coach, Robert Deveau. Coach Deveau lived in an old apartment in town and drove an old car. He dressed in sweatpants and a sweatshirt. Coach Deveau wasn't successful in my father's mind, so there was no way I'd tell my father my goal was to be just like him.

During my senior year at Putnam High School (PHS), Worcester Polytechnic Institute (WPI) and the University of Connecticut (UCONN) recruited me to play football. WPI was an engineering school whose head football coach, Bob Weiss, was a Putnam High School graduate. Dick Reilly, the defensive coordinator for UCONN, stopped by PHS to talk to both myself and my good friend, offensive tackle Bart Ramos. He offered us walk-on positions if we selected UCONN for our academic studies.

As high school graduation loomed closer, my physics teacher, Dr. Louise Pempek, asked to speak to me after school. Dr. Pempek was a UCONN graduate with a doctorate in physics and was simply the best teacher at Putnam High. Not only was Dr. Pempek an extremely caring person, but she could also make the complex simple when it came to teaching her students. She loved what she did, and her enthusiasm was truly contagious. I had no idea why she wanted to talk to me after school, but I was about to find out.

I can still remember walking into her classroom and receiving a big friendly smile. She asked me to have a seat next to her desk. Dr. Pempek started the conversation. She said, "Craig, I've heard from our guidance counselor you have selected engineering as the major you wish to pursue in college, and that both UCONN and WPI have expressed interest in having you play football for them. I want to congratulate you on the hard work and dedication you've shown in the classroom and on the playing fields here at Putnam High. I've seen firsthand that when you put your mind to something, you accomplish it. The UCONN director of admissions, a close friend of mine, will be coming to our class later this month. He can accept students on the spot into the major of their choice."

She continued, "I want you to consider what I have to say before you commit to the major you plan to pursue in college. As you know, I went to UCONN and graduated with my doctorate in physics. I took the same classes as the engineering students during my undergraduate years. I need to be brutally honest with you. I don't think you'll enjoy engineering school. My belief has nothing to do with your ability to graduate as an engineer. I know that if you put your mind to getting a degree in engineering, that's what you'll do. My genuine concern is you aren't going to have any fun with your classmates. You are at the opposite end of the spectrum when it comes to the typical characteristics of a young college engineer. They tend to be nerdy types that breeze through high school academically. They're members of the chess and backgammon clubs, not captains of the football team, dating the school's prettiest girl. May I ask why you've selected engineering as your college major?"

I responded, "My father has been telling me since my elementary school days I need to be an engineer when I grow up. He has a very wealthy friend who is a professional engineer, and my dad wants me to have a life like his."

I remember seeing the sadness in Dr. Pempek's eyes. She said, "Your father has only the best intentions at heart and views success as wealth. Success in life is about doing something you love, not about how much money you make. When you get to do something you love, it never feels like work. It has personal meaning, and you get paid for it. I don't see you enjoying a career as an engineer. You will have to work much harder than your classmates in college, and your reward will be working for a large corporation, sitting in a small cubicle for eight hours a day." I listened intently, all the while secretly agreeing with her.

"What do you recommend?" I asked.

She replied, "Let's think outside the box. If I were you, I would apply to the School of Drama at NYU. You are a natural actor and leader. You'll have way more fun, and I believe you'll find a way to have a much larger impact on the world." I sat there in silence. Drama school at NYU? Dr. Pempek clearly didn't understand how things rolled in my family.

I could imagine my father's face when I walked through the door and told him I wanted to be an actor. He would throw me out of the house. But I understood what my favorite teacher was saying. She had a doctorate in physics and was having the time of her life teaching at a small high school in rural Connecticut. I had just received some of the best advice in my life, but I wasn't ready to hear it.

To be truthful, I didn't see myself as an actor in any stage of my life. Even though I still had no idea what an engineer did, I knew it was the only career option that had my father's approval. Deep down, I wanted to be a football coach, but I didn't have the confidence to broach the subject with Dad.

At the end of the month, the UCONN director of admissions came to our physics college preparatory class and sat behind Dr. Pempek's desk. One by one, each student approached the desk and gave their SAT score, class rank, and major of choice. I approached the desk and said, "1,080, twelfth in my class, mechanical engineering." The admissions director replied, "Craig, your SAT score is below immediate acceptance levels into the School of Engineering." Then he looked toward Dr. Pempek, who calmly stated, "If Craig says he wants to be an engineer, he'll graduate as an outstanding engineer."

The director looked back at me and penciled in "School of Engineering" on my application. He did the same for one of my best friends, Steve Chenail, who got accepted into the School of Physical Therapy. My college experience was about to begin. Steve and I were going to be freshman roommates at UCONN.

Without understanding what I had just done, I jumped on Society's Path with the rest of the herd. It happens to so many of us. We listen to the people we are conditioned to trust, and we blindly do what everyone else is doing. We attend college, land an excellent corporate job, and begin the lifelong process of trying to impress someone in the corner office and climb the ladder of success. Little did I realize how hard it is to change your course once you get on this Path.

I was concerned about the difficulty of engineering school and decided not to walk-on to the UCONN football team my first semester. I would concentrate on getting accustomed to dormitory living and doing well academically. Steve and I were typical college freshmen, living on a campus that had a legal drinking age of 18. We studied hard from Sunday night through Wednesday night, and then partied at dormitory keg parties every Thursday night. UCONN was primarily a commuter's campus back then, so the parties happened the night before much of campus went home on Fridays.

The decision to focus on my studies paid off. I finished my first semester at UCONN with a 2.85 GPA. But Dr. Pempek had been correct. I was usually the last person studying in our dorm's cafeteria each night, and the students in my classes were nothing like the friends and teammates I had in high school.

I missed playing football that first fall semester. Many of the top players I had competed against in high school had been given full scholarships to UCONN. I went to a couple of the home games that first fall semester and sat in the stands at Memorial Stadium. Goose bumps covered me at every game. Not the ones you get when you're cold. The kind you get when a higher power is talking to you! Throughout that first semester, I couldn't stop thinking about playing football at UCONN.

Over the holiday break, I informed my parents I planned to walk-on during the spring semester. I met with my high school football coach and let him know my intentions. Coach Deveau was very supportive. He gave me a key to his office and access to the high school gym and strength equipment. I went to the gym every day during the school break to lift weights and run sprints.

I remember how nervous I was during my first day back on campus as I walked to the Field House's football offices. I played high school football at 5′ 7″ and 155 pounds. I was a small kid hoping to play college football at the 1-AA level. My hands were sweating when I reached the administrative assistant at the football office's entrance. I asked to speak to Dick Reilly.

Coach Reilly came around the corner with a big smile and hand extended, and walked me to his office. When he heard I was there to take him up on his offer to walk-on to the football team, he excitedly introduced me to the head football coach, Walt Nadzak. Coach Nadzak shook my hand, welcomed me to the team, and gave me a copy of the spring conditioning program that would begin in the ROTC hangar the following week. He asked me to start attending the weekly Sunday team meeting. At this level, football was a year-round sport. I let him know I would be there and walked back to my dorm, covered in goose bumps and smiling from ear to ear.

I'll never forget my introduction to the team that Sunday night. Coach Nadzak stood at the podium in front of the room and started the meeting by welcoming the team back from the holiday break. He then let everyone know he was adding a new player to the roster, a walk-on from Putnam, Connecticut. He placed a small blue plastic toy on the podium, which proceeded to walk across the desktop when released from his hand.

"Please welcome Smurf! I mean, Craig Perkins, to the team!" It was a small blue plastic wind-up Smurf, and Coach Nadzak had set my nickname in stone! The room erupted in laughter, and everyone high-fived me. I was finally back in my element. I worked extremely hard in the weight room and on the practice field, and won starting positions on various special teams during the fall season. I knew I would never play beyond the college level, but I loved everything about the sport of football.

Toward the end of my sophomore year, I learned from friends that many other engineering schools had implemented a cooperative education system where engineering students took an entire semester off to work at an engineering company. The goal was to get real-world experience in the field. UCONN had not implemented such a program at that time, but I felt I needed to participate for a couple of reasons. First, the experience would look excellent on a résumé and would certainly help me land a job upon graduation. Second, and more important to me, it would help me understand what being an engineer would be like in the real world.

It was time for another tough decision. Would my coaches allow me to take time off from the football team? Would I lose my eligibility to play when I came back to campus? I was a starter on special teams but only a fourth-string running back on the depth charts. I loved playing football and didn't want to lose my position on the team for good. We had a new head coach, Tom Jackson, and an entirely new coaching staff. I met with Coach Jackson and my running backs coach, Rusty Burns. I explained my dilemma and was relieved when they were supportive of my decision to give the co-op a try. They assured me I would still have my spot on the team when I came back to campus.

So, instead of returning to campus at the beginning of my junior year, I headed to Danbury, Connecticut, to begin my six-month cooperative education experience at Perkin-Elmer. Much to my delight, I found out I would be working on the optical control system of the Hubble Space Telescope. I found a small second-floor apartment in a sweet older woman's home not far from the facility and moved in my essentials, with my barbell and bench being highest on the list. It would become my living space and home gym Monday through Friday for the next six months.

I worked under Paul Yettito, manager of the optical control system of the Hubble Space Telescope. During my first day, I was given a tour of the giant facility. They also showed me how to put on a clean suit and move through the sequential clean rooms before entering the large assembly room for the Hubble's primary mirror. It was a fantastic initial experience for an upcoming young engineer. I was given a desk and chair in my tiny cubicle in the middle of the vast engineering department. For the next six months, I performed various engineering calculations to determine the correct placement of servomotors based on the forces required to adjust the primary mirror's shape.

I quickly learned that sitting in a cubicle for eight hours a day was its own type of torture. It was fantastic to put on a clean suit, pass through the vacuum chambers, and see the actual mirror headed for deep space, but sitting at my desk in a cubicle was boring as hell. In this environment, the thought of being an engineer for the rest of my life started losing its luster. I could do the work, but it wasn't that gratifying. Meetings filled my days, where very little got accomplished.

The facility overflowed with engineers and technicians who seemed fine with doing their little piece of the project, getting paid well, and leaving promptly when the clock hit 4:00 p.m. I did my job well and got a glowing review from my boss, but I couldn't wait for the six months to end. Upon returning to campus and the practice fields at UCONN, Dr. Pempek's words kept echoing in my mind. Was engineering really what I wanted to do for the rest of my life? I tried to focus and get back to studying and practicing hard. But the thoughts wouldn't go away. The co-op provided a real-world experience of what life would be like as an engineer, and it didn't give me goose bumps.

Deep within my soul, I still knew what I wanted to do when I grew up. In high school, I wanted to be a gym teacher and head football coach. After playing football at the college level, my dream shifted to becoming a college-level football coach. Taking this Path would require transferring to the School of Education and gathering the credentials to start as a high school physical education teacher.

I agonized over this decision. I knew this required going against my father's deepest desires. I knew he would be extremely disappointed with me. But in my soul, I needed to coach football. I loved everything about football and the camaraderie that developed from shared suffering under challenging conditions. I loved every element of the male-bonding process and the leadership required to build a team. I loved the weight room and the practice field. Games were fun with the roaring crowds, but I relished the work we needed to do during the week to prepare for play on the weekend. For me, the work was the prize.

For once in my life, it was time for me to listen to myself. It was time to listen to my Authentic Self and embrace what gave me goose bumps. It was time to act like an adult and make my own decisions.

I scheduled a meeting with the assistant dean of Engineering. He was a great guy who always played pickup basketball with the football team in the field house before practice. The day we met to discuss my plans is forever etched in my mind. I was so damn nervous. I was moving toward my fear yet once again. I had made this decision on my own and consulted no one before this meeting. I was determined to follow my passion and become a college-level football coach.

My hands were sweating as I sat in a guest chair outside of his office. My heart was racing, and my mouth was so dry my tongue felt like a piece of rotten wood. When the assistant dean opened his door to greet me, I found myself stumbling for words. He welcomed me with a warm handshake and had me take a seat in his office. "Good morning, Craig. You guys had a great spring football game. You had some great runs from the scrimmage yourself. The team looks good going into next season. It's a lot of fun seeing you out there, Craig, representing the School of Engineering. How may I help you today?"

With trepidation in my voice, I replied, "I've finally figured out what I want to do when I grow up! After working hard in the classroom, on the practice field, and at my recent co-op at Perkin-Elmer, I realize I want to be a college-level football coach and not an engineer. Sitting in a cubicle for eight hours a day just isn't for me. I want to transfer to the School of Education and study to become a high school gym teacher, if that's what it's going to take."

Much to my astonishment, he smiled and said, "Good for you, Craig! I couldn't be happier for you. Many young men and women come to college not knowing what they want to do, and graduate with a degree they never use. Considering your size, having succeeded as a walk-on at this level is an inspiration in itself. I do not doubt you will be an excellent college football coach, and I bet you'll get an internship right here at UCONN. Let me walk you over to the dean of the School of Education and give you a personal introduction."

The assistant dean of Engineering walked me over to the dean of Education, introduced me, and told him my story. The dean of Education seemed as happy as I was. He stuck out his hand and grasped mine. "Welcome to the School of Education, Craig. You are only five semesters into your college education, so it looks like all your classes will count toward your eventual degree in education. Now was the perfect time to make this change. Your workload will be considerably less, and you should be able to focus more on playing football and learning the Xs and Os of the game. The School of Education is proud to have you." I thanked both men and floated back to my dorm. I had made the most significant decision of my life on my own, listening to only my own council. I was proud of who I was becoming.

I finished the semester with final exams, packed up my belongings from my dorm room, and made the 45-minute trip back to my home in Putnam, Connecticut. I was nervous but excited to tell my parents about my new direction in life. After getting things unpacked and settling back into my bedroom at home, I told my parents I needed to talk to them. We sat in the living room, and I began.

"You both know I haven't been overly excited with my engineering classes at college. I work twice as hard as most kids in my classes, and I have never really enjoyed the subjects. Sitting in a cubicle for six months at Perkin-Elmer was enough to make me want to hang myself. My love has always involved team sports, especially football, and I am committed to becoming a college-level football coach after graduation. I have thought long and hard about this over the entire last semester. I met with the assistant dean of

Engineering and the dean of Education, and I've switched to the School of Education. I begin next semester.

"My goal is to get a coaching internship at UCONN upon graduation, but if that doesn't happen, I am willing to become a gym teacher at the high school level and work my way into the college ranks. I know I'll be a great head coach someday!" My mom smiled, and my dad glared. His eyes pierced holes into my soul.

"Craig, you've made a terrible decision. Being a football coach isn't a real career. Look at your old high school football coach and gym teacher. Bob Deveau has never had any real money. He has always lived in an apartment and never owned his own home. He drives a used old vehicle. You are too smart and too driven to have that as your career aspiration. Maybe they pay more at the college level, but it will never amount to the job you would eventually have as an engineer working in a large company. You didn't even have the decency to discuss such a radical change with your mother and me before you made the decision. The only way we will continue to pay for your tuition is if you transfer back into the School of Engineering and continue down the Path you originally set for yourself. Take it or leave it."

My father was disgusted with me, so he got up from his chair and walked outside. This was a lot of pressure for a 21-year-old who had grown up with such a demanding father. All my mother could say was, "You know how much your father has always wanted you to be an engineer. He wants you to make a lot of money and live an easier life." After an entire month of enduring the silent treatment from my father, I buckled. I called and made an appointment with the assistant dean of Engineering. The day I drove back to campus felt like it unfolded in slow motion. I knew I was making the wrong decision, but I felt too much pressure to conform to my father's desires.

When I walked into the assistant dean's office, he could tell something important was at stake. I explained what had happened with my father, and that I needed to switch back to engineering. He looked me in the eye and said, "Craig, I've seen this happen so many times. Parents truly want the best for their kids but fail to realize their job isn't to pick what their kids should do for a living. Their job is to support what their children truly want to do. Many young men and women have no idea what they want to do when they pick a career before college. But you did the work. You came and immersed yourself in your engineering studies, couldn't get past your love for the game of football, and walked onto the team. You figured you might as well do a co-op to see what the real world was really like, and you did just that. With firsthand knowledge, you decided to follow your passion. You did what most of us never accomplish. You figured out what you want to do with your life and decided to follow that Path. Are you sure you want to go back to engineering?"

I looked at the floor and begrudgingly said, "Yes."

Without realizing the long-term implications of this single decision, I did what so many of us do. I listened to the wants and desires of others and jumped back onto Society's Path—the Path that leads to living a life of quiet desperation. If the story of my life reveals nothing more than the overriding importance of listening to your Authentic Self, I've succeeded. Far too many of us listen to those around us and believe they have our best interests at heart. I am here to tell you, most of the people you listen to really don't. Parents, teachers, and even close friends have pre-conceived notions about what success in life should entail. They fail to realize the definition is different for everyone. Society wants us to believe that success means becoming one of the wealthiest people on the block, while living a life of servitude to some large corporation. Learn from me and stop believing the lie.

Even after discovering my Authentic Self, I listened to my father and switched back to the School of Engineering. For the next couple of years, I did my best to combine the work of my engineering classes with the joy of playing football. As I neared the final semester of my college education, I did one of the hardest things I have ever done in my life.

I quit the football team.

I will never forget the day I walked into Head Coach Tom Jackson's office and sat down with him and Coach Burns to let them know I was quitting. I said all the right things. I explained I would never play professional football, and how critical it was to get a good grade on my senior engineering project. My focus needed to be on landing a good job with a Fortune 500 company. My coaches understood and accepted my decision.

I remember Coach Jackson shaking my hand and saying, "Perk, if I owned a company that needed an engineer, you would be the first one I'd hire. You are going to be a terrific employee at any company lucky enough to hire you. Knowing you, you'll be running the company someday. Good luck, and let me know if I can help in any way." I heard the words, but they sounded like they were coming from down the hallway behind three closed doors.

I couldn't believe what I was doing. I barely held back the tears when I stood to shake their hands and walked back outside, where my girlfriend was waiting for me. When Jenny reached out and put her arms around me, I broke down and cried. Right in the middle of campus. I can remember standing on the sidewalk with hundreds of students zigzagging their way to class, and feeling more alone than I had ever felt in my life.

I graduated from UCONN with a bachelor of science in mechanical engineering. Cum laude.

While writing this book, I came across a blog post in my inbox from *Daily Dad* telling a story about the legendary basketball coach Jim Valvano. In the post, Ryan Holiday tells the story of Coach Valvano's unshakable belief in himself, and how he lived his life according to a quote he heard as a kid: "Every single day, in every walk of life, ordinary people accomplish extraordinary things!" Before graduating from high school, Jim told his father, "I am going to be a college basketball coach and win a national championship." We know how my father reacted to a similar statement I made about becoming a college football coach.

That's not how Jim Valvano's dad reacted.

A couple of days after Jim told his dad about his big goal in life, his dad called him into the bedroom and showed Jim a packed suitcase. Jim wondered why his dad had packed. Instead of telling his son that his dreams were unrealistic and he should go to college to get a good education and a high-paying job, Mr. Valvano looked his son in the eyes and said, "I'm packed. When you play and win that National Championship, I'm going to be there, my bags are already packed."

Tears rolled down my face when I read this email. What I

would have given to have a dad like that. How would my life have turned out if it started out with me following my passion? I've learned you must first break the chains tied to others' opinions and start listening to your Authentic Self if you hope to live an Authentic Life.

Remember, the only person you have to impress in life is *yourself*. The only person who can limit the life you want to live stares back at you in the mirror every day. We all know what gives us goose bumps. Society has brainwashed us to be so concerned with what others think, we become terrified that others won't approve of our dreams. So we don't even try.

The **First Guiding Principle** to living an autonomous life is to listen to your Authentic Self. Do whatever it takes to get back in touch with the real you. Then, insert the key, open the damn door, and embrace the hard work ahead.

CHAPTER 2

———

IT'S ALWAYS HARD BEFORE IT'S EASY

"Easy never pays well."

—ANDY FRISELLA

"It's time to get up!" my father yells as he rips the blankets off my bed. "Breakfast will be ready in five. Wash your face and dress in some warm clothes. We've got a lot of wood to cut and haul to the shed today." It's 6:00 a.m. on a cold New England Sunday morning, and the second I try to move, my body hurts everywhere. "What the hell have I done to myself?" I think as I pause in my state of slumber. Then it all comes rushing back to me.

We had a high school football game yesterday where we beat our division rival Somers in the cold, pouring rain.

I ran the ball 40 times for 226 yards and scored three touchdowns. I almost drowned a couple of times in the small ponds that developed on the field. My body felt like a piñata at the end of a fourth-grade birthday party.

It was a typical fall Sunday at the Perkins household during my high school years. My father, brother, and I would spend from dawn till dusk cutting the treetops left from the professional loggers who had harvested hardwood from our 63 acres. While my father and brother used chainsaws to cut the large limbs into five-foot lengths, I used my back and body to load them into the trailer attached to our Kubota tractor.

Once we delivered them to our woodshed, we attached the cord saw to the tractor, and we cut the logs into 15-inch lengths. Then, we attached the hydraulic wood splitter and split any large logs before we stacked everything under the open-air woodshed that my father, brother, and I had built with our own hands. Twelve cord of wood got cut, split, and stacked every fall to burn in the two woodstoves we used to help heat our home during the cold winter months and reduce our electric bill.

I learned at a young age life wasn't going to be easy.

My brother and I had what can be best described as an employee/employer relationship with our father. Hard work was the foundation of our upbringing. My brother still calls it slave labor. Dad was a perfectionist, and we did our chores under his watchful eye. Good enough was never enough. While we never developed a loving relationship with our father, he did teach us the value of hard work. We learned one of the most important lessons anyone can understand:

Success in life is always on the other side of hard work.

Anything new is difficult. From taking your first few steps as a child to learning how to ride a bike, it's always hard before it gets easy. We all learn this life lesson, but at some point, many of us forget it. We find a little comfort and latch onto it. A good-paying job, a lovely house in the suburbs, and recreational fun on the weekends. We trade our Freedom for a false sense of security and believe the hard work is finally over. We should all know better.

Comfort never lasts forever. The market crashes, the company we work for gets sold, someone within our family is stricken with an unforeseen illness. The work required to survive comes back instantly, but our bodies and minds have become soft from lounging around in the comfort of Society's Box.

> Do you *really* want to find your Freedom? Do you want the autonomy to live each day on your terms? Then you'd better embrace the work required to get you there and keep you there. If you are on the correct Path in life, work never goes away. Having the discipline to put work before pleasure is the **Second Guiding Principle** for finding your Freedom.

Retired Navy SEAL Jocko Willink clearly explains this fundamental truth in his book *Discipline Equals Freedom: Field Manual.* I highly recommend reading this book and understanding how injecting discipline into your daily routines leads to greater personal Freedom, not less.

My life throughout high school centered on work. I worked hard to get good grades and excel as a student. I worked just as hard to excel as an athlete, parking my student identity in the locker room corner, suiting up, and practicing hard for whatever sport was currently in season. Then I showered, ate my brown-bag dinner and drove to work at the Ford dealership my father managed, where I swept up the speedy-dry and dumped all the garbage from the service department.

Work wasn't complete until I cleaned all the restrooms and mopped the entire sales department's floor. I usually got home around 8:00 p.m. and set up shop on my father's large wooden desk in the basement to do my homework. Mom always yelled for me to go to bed at 11:00 p.m. I repeated this process day after day. Success in every area of my life hinged on putting in the necessary work.

When I moved away to college, my commitment to work got me through my freshman year. I may not have been the smartest engineer accepted into UCONN, but I was undoubtedly one of the hardest working. I was always one of the last remaining students studying in our dorm's cafeteria each night. Deciding to walk-on to the football team during my second semester as an engineering student only increased the amount of work it would take to succeed.

When everyone else went to the Thursday night keg parties across campus, I found a private cubicle at the Homer Babbidge Library to study. I became an expert in time management, combining engineering school and football. The discipline I had learned at a young age of putting work before pleasure continued to pay dividends in my life.

My relationship with work further intensified when I landed my first job as a manufacturing engineer with the Torrington Company. I may have given up on my dream of coaching college football, but I approached my first job out of UCONN with the same dedication and enthusiasm I would have had if I were coaching a football team.

I found myself standing in the middle of a century-old unionized manufacturing plant with an embedded "us versus them" mentality between management and the union. Management's philosophy was to have the workers park their brains at the plant entrance and just do what their managers told them to do. If you wore a tie and touched a piece of equipment, a union grievance would be sitting on your desk before the end of the day. Due to the ingrained culture within this old factory, most of the engineers I worked with were more focused on where they were going for lunch and their plans for the upcoming weekend than how they could improve the Standard Plant's performance.

By 3:30 p.m., most salaried workers were back in their second-floor cubicles anxiously watching the clock as it crept toward 4:00 p.m. If you got caught in the hallway when the clock struck 4:00 p.m., the stampede of people pouring out the doors would run over you! I was never part of that herd. I relished when the clock hit 4:00. Most of the distractions were gone, and I could focus on completing the tasks I had set for the day. Plant management noticed my work ethic early on, which played an integral role in my advancement.

Less than a year after joining the Standard Plant team, the Torrington Company's president issued an ultimatum that pushed this old unionized plant to improve its performance. Our president, Tom Bennett, told the Standard Plant management team to focus on one product line in the factory and do whatever was required to reach the newly defined "World-Class" manufacturing levels of:

- 100 percent schedule attainment
- Less than 1 percent production defects
- 50-plus Work-In-Process (WIP) inventory turns

There was a lot at stake for the Standard Plant, one of the last remaining unionized factories in the company. Bringing a product line to world-class manufacturing levels was a last-ditch effort to prove the old plant still had what it took to be competitive in the new worldwide marketplace. The Standard Plant management team selected the pump vane manufacturing cell to prove we had what it took. I was assigned to the pump vane cell to see if I could help the product line reach world-class manufacturing levels. I finally had a team to lead!

Teamwork starts with trust, and the pump vane workers needed to trust the new kid who was wearing a tie and asking many questions. They needed to believe I was committed to helping them succeed, so I started coming to work at 5:00 a.m. to meet with the third shift workers before their shift ended. Then, I stayed past 5:00 p.m. to ensure all three shifts communicated directly with me daily. My philosophy of improvement centered on coaching and teamwork. I never forgot the advice my grandfather had given me: "Listen to the person doing the job." I became obsessed with helping the pump vane cell reach world-class manufacturing levels and proving we could do it in this old unionized plant.

It took months to develop the trust needed to get the operators to tell me what they thought was wrong. Slowly but surely, they realized I was there to stay. I was committed to helping them reach the goals that had been set for us. I was the facilitator and coach alongside their foreman, Don Aube, one of the management guys left at the plant who was a rare champion of his workers. Each time we improved the manufacturing process's capability, the defect level dropped, schedule attainment improved, and the team grew tighter. After 24 months of hard work and long hours, the pump vane department posted the following improvements:

- Schedule attainment improved from 65 to 100 percent
- Defects reduced from 12.1 to .5 percent
- WIP inventory turns increased from 25 to 55

Our 17-person pump vane team won the prestigious President's Award, and my career shifted into high gear. Together, we forged our process of workforce ownership. We implemented more manufacturing cells throughout the plant, combined them with self-directed work teams, and created success after success in that old unionized factory. It was a ton of work, but I was obsessed with keeping the plant open.

Instead of coaching football players, I coached groups of UAW workers and young engineers. I was following my

Purpose. As an entry-level engineer in a 50,000-square-foot unionized factory, the impossible progressed from winning the President's Award to becoming the cell manufacturing superintendent, and finally the plant manager. After nine years of complex and challenging work, a joint UAW/Standard Plant management system ran the factory. No one would have ever deemed it possible. Those were some of the best years of my life, and my reward is the close group of friends from the Standard Plant I still have to this day.

When upper management put the Standard Plant under a new division that still believed the union was the enemy, all the fun came to a screeching halt. In an instant, the joy of my job evaporated. What used to be Freedom at work suddenly felt like prison. I needed to get out or risk becoming one of the mummies filled with Corporate America's embalming fluid. I kicked down the walls of Society's Box and wiped the slate clean. I quit my job as plant manager and started Islands of Success Management Consulting.

After two years of consulting for small manufacturing companies and yearning for a business of my own, I found a 12,000-square-foot World Gym for sale about an hour away from where I lived. I wiped the slate clean once again. I cashed in my 401(k), borrowed money from my good friend and consulting partner, Elliot, and bought the gym for $318,600. I never imagined how much work being an entrepreneur would entail, but I was passionate about fitness and obsessed with being my own boss.

For the first time in my life, everything was on the line. I was "all in" with the purchase of World Gym. My first wife, Gina, and I had $10,000 left to our names. Gina kept her job as a cook at a convalescent home to maintain some household income, and helped at the gym whenever she could. Elliot came on as the office manager and handled accounting for the new business. There was no escape hatch for me this time around. The gym had to succeed, or I was going to go broke.

The hours were long—longer than I had ever worked before. Six employees covered all the hours when I first purchased the gym. Both cleanliness and customer service were lacking. I jumped right in to fill any voids at the front counter. I started working from 9:30 a.m. to 10:30 p.m. on weekdays, and 7:00 a.m. to 3:00 p.m. on the weekends. I worked more than 75 hours a week to help cover the schedule, ensuring we had the basics covered. The gym came before anything else in my life. I was living the entrepreneur's dream!

I hope I am getting my point across. If you want to be free, you *must* be willing to put in the work. Nothing else matters. If the idea of working 80 hours for yourself for the first two or three years—so you don't have to work 40 hours for someone else—doesn't resonate with your soul, stay in the cage Society has built for you. Merely wanting something different is never enough. You need to *welcome* the tremendous amount of work it will take to try and make the change.

For some strange reason, as we become adults, we forget what it takes to get better at something in life. When we are young, we don't even think about how complicated it is to get better. We know we want to do something we've never tried before, and we know it's not going to be easy.

For example, when I was young, I fell in love with baseball. Every time I watched a game on television, the rest of the world melted away. When my father took our family to a Red Sox game at Fenway Park, goose bumps covered my body. I knew in my soul I needed to try and play this game. When I started, I had no idea how to swing a bat or catch a ball. But that didn't deter me. I didn't listen to anyone who tried to tell me that baseball was too hard, a dumb idea, too expensive, a boring game, or whatever else to deter me from the Path I was pursuing. I just embraced the work of getting better.

My dad got me a bat, a glove, and some balls, along with a batting stick and a rebounding backstop. He showed me how to hold the bat, swing on a level plane, and throw and field the ball. From there, success was up to me. It's the same for all of us.

It all comes down to a simple yet difficult decision: Do we embrace the work of getting better? Do we put in the practice? If we do, something magical happens along the way. If the new activity resonates with our soul, practice turns into play, and we improve. If the new activity never touches our soul, practice turns into work, and we quickly lose interest in getting better.

When the motivation to get better is intrinsic, we grab that bat and swing it for hours on end. The more work we put into swinging the bat, the better we get at hitting the ball. The more we throw the ball into the rebounder and field the pop-ups and grounders, the better we become at throwing and fielding. If we stay committed to the work, we continue to improve.

It was that simple. It *is* that simple.

But as adults, we forget how this process of improvement works. We start believing progress can happen without putting in the work. We think we can read the latest motivational book or watch the latest motivational video, and poof! We are on our way to reaching our goals. I'm sorry to tell you: you can *never* skip the work.

Once you have determined what gives you goose bumps, success and reaching your goals is always on the other side of hard work. The key is embracing the hard work and looking forward to the mundane tasks associated with getting better. I embraced getting up and cutting wood all day on the weekends throughout my high school years because I wanted to be a better football player. I knew the process of lifting five-foot hardwood logs was making me functionally stronger.

Finding Freedom in life follows a very similar Path of putting work before pleasure.

My love for the game of football didn't stop when I graduated from high school. I made the difficult decision to walk-on to the UCONN football team while attending engineering school. While everyone thought it was awesome I played football at college, most never saw the work required behind the scenes. I stayed up till 1:00 a.m. studying for an important exam, then hopped out of bed at 6:00 a.m. to be at the field house for conditioning. This was a regular part of my college existence. I was willing to do the work required to be on the playing field because I didn't want to sit in the bleachers with the spectators.

My commitment to work continued after graduating from college. Working more than 60 hours per week at the Standard Plant and being a visible leader on all three production shifts of the pump vane cell created the spark that ignited change in the "us versus them" culture in that old unionized manufacturing plant. Purchasing a failing gym and working 75 hours per week or more to ensure we survived came next. Every time something good happened in my life, it was due to the tremendous amount of work I put in.

I owned that gym for 17 years. I enjoyed a life filled with autonomy. And just when it felt like the hard work was finally over, I received a letter by certified mail explaining my franchise agreement would only renew if I spent close to $2 million to move and expand my existing location.

You guessed it. I wiped the slate clean once again. I left the comfort of owning my gym to become a new Sola Salon Studio franchisee with my second wife, Stephanie. I finally understood the relationship between hard work and autonomy. Work is the fuel that powers the bus. But why the hell was I starting over again?! The answer was simple: to keep the Freedom I'd worked so hard to obtain.

So started the two-year grind with Stephanie to find our first Sola location in New Hampshire. We had to overcome the problems and mistakes that were made during our first construction process. But we kept our noses to the grindstone, did the work, and finally saw the faces of our new renters light up when they moved into their boutique salons and opened their own businesses! The level of success you enjoy in life boils down to the amount of hard work and suffering that precedes it. Please embrace this fact. It's what separates the few from the herd.

Take an honest look at your life thus far. Have you embraced hard work? When you were young, did you do your weekly chores even though you didn't want to, or were you constantly yelled at and punished for not getting them done? Did you get your homework done before playing with your neighborhood friends or jumping on your iPad? Did you play sports and work as hard in practice as you did during the actual games? At work, do you willingly put in whatever hours are required to get the job done on time? Ask yourself this question:

> Even if this book gave you all the answers you were looking for, would your unwillingness to do the work stop you from moving forward?

If you've gotten too comfortable in your current life, and you avoid the work required to find Freedom, work to build your mental toughness before trying to break out of Society's Box. Remember, it's hard to leave the herd. It's hard mentally to stop listening to the naysayers. It's hard financially to take steps backward in terms of reliable income. It's hard physically because of the tremendous amount of work it requires to master any new skill. It's hard emotionally because it always takes twice as long as you think to reach your goals. There is nothing easy about going Against the Grain and trying to live an Authentic Life.

Embrace the fact that creating a life filled with autonomy

is difficult. The struggle is the test to see if you have the will to become your Authentic Self. Change implies "doing." Most people never make the jump from having a plan to *doing the work* to implement the plan. Creating autonomy in your life requires embracing the hard work necessary to master anything new. But even if you have the confidence to follow a new Path in life and welcome the tremendous amount of work it will take to reach your goals, there is still another obstacle standing between you and your Freedom. Without a clear Vision of what Freedom means to *you*, it's almost impossible to create a life filled with autonomy.

CHAPTER 3

WHAT'S YOUR VISION OF FREEDOM?

"The purpose of life, as far as I can tell...is to find a mode of being that's so meaningful that the fact that life is suffering is no longer relevant."

—JORDAN PETERSON

In the movie *Fight Club*, Tyler Durden walks into a 24-hour convenience store and places a gun to the cashier's head. "Give me your wallet," Tyler says as he presses the gun against the man's temple. With the clerk's license in hand, Tyler reads off the name and address: "Raymond K. Hessel, 1329 SE Benning, Apartment A." Finding an expired student ID card in the wallet, Tyler asks, "What did you want to be, Raymond K. Hessel?" Tyler cocks the pistol.

"The question, Raymond. What did you want to be?" Raymond, much to our relief, finally gives Tyler an answer. A vet. He wanted to be a veterinarian but gave up because it was too hard, and there was too much school. Tyler, still holding the gun to Raymond's head, makes a promise: if Raymond isn't back in school by the time he returns in a year, he's going to kill him.

I wish this would happen to all of us! Most of us would be living a very different life if we were forced to be honest about what we genuinely wanted to do. Although this book doesn't come "locked and loaded" with live ammunition, I hope it provides an experience similar to what Raymond K. Hessel endured. I hope this book helps open your eyes before you waste most of your life chasing Society's lies. I consider myself one of the lucky ones. I was only 32 when I had the proverbial gun placed to my head.

After eight years of working my way up Society's Ladder in my first job out of college, I accepted the plant manager position for a century-old United Auto Workers (UAW) organized manufacturing plant that had over 500 employees. One day as I was doing my daily morning walk through the factory, I received a page from my secretary. Teresa told me our division's vice president needed to talk to me by phone at the top of the hour. I let Teresa know I was headed back to my office. My joint management team with UAW Local 1645 had recently developed a five-year improvement plan for the Standard Plant and sent it to corporate for their approval. I was hoping this phone call was the "yes" we needed to implement our plan.

My first job after graduating as a mechanical engineer from UCONN was with the Torrington Company. The Torrington Company manufactured bearings for the Big 3 American automakers. I started at the Standard Plant as a young project engineer, and within three years, my superiors promoted me to cell manufacturing superintendent. My success at the plant stemmed from my desire to be a head football coach rather than an engineer. I learned my most valuable business skills from playing team sports, not from sitting in a classroom. I believed in people, not in numbers. I was a champion of the shop floor worker, and I did everything I could to put the workers in charge of their workplace.

Our company had recently purchased a competitor that produced bearings for the airline industry. Some of the factories were closed during the acquisition, and their product lines transferred into our facilities. We had recently moved numerous product lines from one of the closed factories into the Standard Plant.

The aircraft product transfer and integration into the Standard Plant had not gone well. The new product lines were killing the factory. The failure to successfully manage the transfer cost our plant manager his job. When upper management offered me his position, I initially turned it down. I wanted nothing to do with the mess that had been created. But our local UAW leadership convinced me I needed to take the position if the factory had any hope of surviving. It was a lot of pressure for a 32-year-old young man.

I made it clear to my superiors that accepting the plant manager's job was contingent on the Standard Plant staying under the control of my existing Automotive Division. I had met the upper management team from the Aircraft Division, and I wanted nothing to do with them. They were dinosaurs from the past and were known for terrible worker relations and numerous union strikes. My success at the plant stemmed from creating a joint management team with our UAW Local 1645 leaders. My manager promised me the Standard Plant would stay under the Automotive Division if I accepted the plant manager position.

So, I accepted the position. The Standard Plant was losing around $1 million a month. In my first six months as plant manager, our joint management team made great strides in getting the factory back to breakeven, saving the plant from losing the million dollars each month. We accomplished the improvements by doing something never done before in the plant's history: union leadership temporarily allowed skilled tradesmen to run the production equipment transferred in from the closed factory. The skilled tradesmen quickly solved the production problems, building new tooling on the spot.

We eventually worked our way through the backlog of orders. We needed approval from upper management to implement our five-year improvement plan so we could bring all the product lines produced within the Standard Plant to world-class manufacturing levels.

But the ring of the phone startled me.

"Hello, Craig. It's Jack. Are you alone in your office?" I was confused. The vice president of personnel, Jack, was at the other end of the call, not the VP of my division. Jack let me know my current division's VP, Alan, and the new Aircraft Division's VP, Steve, were also on the line. Alan and Steve said hello. It didn't take a rocket scientist to figure out that change was coming. Without even a thank you for getting the plant back to breakeven, Jack let me know that the Standard Plant was now under the Aircraft Division's management. My new boss would be Jerry, the operations manager of the Aircraft Division. Blood rushed to my feet. My heart was beating so fast it felt like it was going to explode.

I objected and reminded everyone of the promises made when I accepted the plant manager position. Alan stammered and said, "I'm sorry, Craig, but it's time to let the Aircraft Division solve the problems created when their product lines transferred into the Standard Plant. Steve and Jerry believe they can return the plant to profitability without spending anywhere near the capital in your five-year plan." I was speechless when I hung up the phone. I looked out my window at the packed parking lot below and wondered how to tell the union. What would I say to Barry Bayly, my business partner at the Standard Plant, and shop chairman for UAW Local 1645?

In an instant, everything we had worked so hard for over the past eight years was coming undone. I knew it in my bones.

At my first meeting with my new boss, Jerry, he sat across from my desk and said, "Craig, I know you've made great progress in many areas of this factory, but I believe you've become too close with the union. From what I can tell from my plant tour, the workers no longer understand who the bosses are. Managers manage, workers work. That's how things get done in this company." My heart missed some beats. The Freedom I once had to get things done under my old division had suddenly evaporated. Jerry proposed *his* plan to bring the plant back to profitability. It involved laying off the skilled tradesmen who had just fixed most of the production problems with the new aircraft product lines. I was dumbfounded.

"Jerry," I stated, "you want me to lay off the workers who just saved this plant's ass?!"

He responded, "If skilled tradesmen have the time to run production equipment, they don't have enough of their own work to do. They are the highest-paid hourly workers in the entire company. It's time we start looking at outsourcing the toolmaking done at the plant to reduce our operating costs." It had taken me eight years to get managers and workers to realize they were on the same team. Jerry's plan would destroy what I had put my heart and soul into creating.

I refused to implement his plan. I drew a line in the sand, and Jerry knew he couldn't just fire me. The union would likely walk off the job if he did.

A day or two later, Jerry called me down to his office and let me know he wasn't going to push the layoffs immediately. Instead, the Standard Plant would implement an old-school management system for controlling spending. As far as Jerry was concerned, If I wasn't going to lay off workers and reduce payroll, we needed to drastically cut the plant's spending to return it to profitability. I knew we were on the wrong Path because it's virtually impossible to "save" your way to profitability.

After a couple of months of working under Jerry, he asked my wife and me to dinner. Jerry wanted us to "get to know each other better." He knew we had a poor relationship. It was the last thing I wanted to do, but we met Jerry and his wife at a local restaurant on a Saturday night. Little did I know, this dinner would be my proverbial "Last Supper" with the Torrington Company.

Jerry's ego controlled the conversation throughout dinner. He bragged that no one at the Torrington Company worked longer hours than he did. Jerry explained that his wife understood the need for all the hours. His goal was to become an executive vice president at the company, but his kids always complained they didn't see him enough.

Jerry's voice suddenly got serious, and he looked me straight in the eye. "I finally solved the problem for my kids. I taped a life-sized picture of myself to the front of our refrigerator and told my kids they can see me anytime now!" The grin that came across his face was disturbing. The realization he was being honest disgusted me.

Jerry had placed the proverbial gun to my head.

I left dinner knowing my career with the Torrington Company was over. I couldn't work much longer for such a fool of a man, and I didn't trust my former division after they lied to me when I accepted the plant manager position. It was my time to answer Tyler Durden's question: "What do you really want to do with your life, Craig Perkins?"

At 32 years of age, I had come to a critical juncture in my life. It would be easiest to accept my new reality and embrace the Path most employees follow: shut your mouth and do what your boss tells you so you can keep your high-paying job and continue to afford a lifestyle designed to keep up with the Joneses. I never wanted to be some corporate minion. I had followed the dreams of my father. The longer I tried to swim in the embalming fluid of Corporate America, the more disgusted I became with the person staring back at me in the mirror.

I decided to perform the ultimate act of Freedom. I quit.

My answer to Tyler Durden's question? I wanted to own my own business. Little did I know then, but the real struggles in my life were about to begin. I had quit based primarily on emotion, without considering where I truly wanted to go. I jumped off Society's Path without ever building the stool to reach the key required to unlock the door to my Authentic Life. No matter how hard I tried to turn the handle, the damn door wouldn't open.

I didn't have a Purpose, so I couldn't open the door.

It took me years of struggle to finally figure that out. It would be best if you didn't struggle the way I did. I don't want you to suffer through a divorce, get lured down less-than-ideal paths to great wealth and status, or partner with people who don't have the same goals and values you do. I've experienced them all and have the scars to show for it. I wrote this book to help others realize there is a way out of the box Society tries to lock us in. I know. I've been there and escaped. Once you have decided to go Against the Grain, there is a methodology that will significantly improve your chances of success. The journey starts with answering a fundamental question only you can answer:

What's your Vision of Freedom?

James Altucher does an excellent job describing Freedom in his blog post, "My 10 Commandments of Freedom." His explanation provides a perfect framework to help you create your Vision of Freedom. If you don't know where you are going, it's a sure bet you'll never get there. I've listed his five Freedoms below and summarized my take on each one. Start by building the first leg of your stool: create your Vision of Freedom.

1. Freedom from health concerns. (Don't be a prisoner of your body.)
2. Freedom from money concerns. (Don't be a prisoner of your bank account.)
3. Freedom from outcomes. (Don't be a prisoner of unreasonable goals or Society's expectations.)
4. Freedom from validation. (Don't be a prisoner of other people's opinions.)
5. Freedom from toxic people. (Don't be a prisoner of those closest to you.)

Grab an empty notepad. Jot down some personal notes. Where does your life currently stand concerning each type of Freedom? Rate yourself on a scale of 1 (worst) to 10 (best).

Freedom from Health Concerns. This type of Freedom trumps all others. If you aren't in good health, all the other kinds of Freedom become meaningless. It doesn't have to be a terminal illness. Being an insulin-dependent diabetic removes some of your daily Freedom. It's not easy to overcome bad genetics, but take a hard look at your current state of health. Do you exercise for at least 30 minutes daily? Do you stay away from sugar and processed carbs as much as you can, and eat whole foods that come from either hunting or harvesting? Do you get at least seven to eight hours of quality sleep each night? Do you currently take prescription medications for an ongoing medical problem? Don't be a prisoner of your body. Rate your current *Freedom from Health Concerns* on a scale from 1–10. What would you need to do to reach a rating of 9–10? Jot down a list in your notebook.

Freedom from Money Concerns. Financial Freedom, or Freedom from money concerns, is as simple as it sounds, but very difficult to embrace. If you consistently spend less than you make, you have mastered the foundation of financial Freedom. Do you have an accurate monthly budget of all household revenue and expenses? Do you check each week to see where you stand? Do you have enough medical and life insurance to cover a personal catastrophe? Are you saving at least 10–15 percent of your income each month for retirement? Do you still have extra money to pursue activities that bring joy to your life? Rate your *Freedom from Money Concerns* on a scale from 1–10. What would you need to do to reach a rating of 9–10?

Freedom from Outcomes. Do you always need to win to feel validated for your efforts? Does being bad at something, only because you haven't done it before, deter you from putting in the work to get better? Freedom comes from being addicted to the process of getting better, not from the goal of winning the race. You only have control of the process, never the outcomes. I never focused on being an All-State running back in high school. I focused on putting in the work each day at practice and in the weight room to get stronger, faster, and more knowledgeable. I never focused on becoming plant manager when I started as a young manufacturing engineer. I focused on creating trust and teamwork on the shop floor, and improving the product line's performance. Don't be a prisoner to Society's expectations. Rate your current *Freedom from Outcomes* on a scale from 1–10. What would you need to do to reach a rating of 9–10?

Freedom from Validation. Are you overly concerned with fitting in with a particular crowd? Do you dream of having a street named after you in your hometown? Do you need to live in a specific town, with the most prominent house, driving only certain brands of automobiles? The need for approval plays the most significant role in keeping people stuck in Society's Box. We are hardwired to fit in with the group. In the early days of mankind, we lived and survived in small groups. Not fitting in could have meant being ostracized from the group and potential death. Today, validation has gone so far in the wrong direction that people have their feelings hurt by someone they've never even met on social media! People stay stuck in unfulfilling lives and jobs because they fear what people will say if they take a different Path. Don't be a prisoner of other people's opinions. Rate your current *Freedom from Validation* on a scale from 1–10. What would you need to do to reach a rating of 9–10?

Freedom from Toxic People. Most of us don't realize toxic people are an impenetrable barrier to Freedom. These people can be family members and close friends. They can be hard to uncover, but eventually, they reveal themselves. These people never say the words "Great job!" when you succeed at something they aren't capable of doing. It's someone who will never say, "Good luck with your plan. If you need anything on your journey, ask, and I will do whatever I can to help." These are the people that bristle when you talk about taking a new Path and say, "Are you crazy? That is way too risky!" It's hard enough to silence our internal critics when we try to move down a different Path, but having toxic people in your inner circle will stop you in your tracks. Don't be a prisoner of the ones closest to you. Rate your current state of *Freedom from Toxic People* from 1–10. What would you need to do to reach a rating of 9–10?

Organize your answers into a collective whole, and you're looking at a solid draft of your Vision of Freedom. Read it as a complete document, and you may identify some things that don't ring entirely true for you. You may see places where you weren't completely honest in your answers. That's okay. Take some time to revise it until it is precisely what you want your future to look like. Rewrite it a bunch of times if you need to. Read it aloud to yourself day after day. Take the time to let it ferment. Without having a clear Vision of what Freedom means to you, it's almost impossible to get where you think you are going. Once it becomes clear, stand back and admire your handiwork. You've successfully built the first leg of your three-legged stool.

I wrote this book to be the proverbial gun to your head. I wrote it to wake you up from your slumber and help you live your life more authentically. I wrote it to help you figure out what truly matters to you so you can put in the work on a daily basis to create a life that gives *you* the Freedom to pursue your Purpose with the people you love and respect. Now that you know what Freedom means to you, the next step to building your stool centers on uncovering your Purpose.

Start thinking about what gives you goose bumps.

CHAPTER 4

WHAT GIVES YOU GOOSE BUMPS?

"Don't ask what the world needs. Ask what makes you come alive, and go do it. Because what the world needs is people who have come alive."

—HOWARD THURMAN

A good friend once said to me, "When you get goose bumps, listen, because God is talking to you." I remember the times throughout my younger years when I watched a great movie like *Rocky* or listened to a coach give a pep talk before a big game, and goose bumps suddenly covered my arms. A feeling of pure happiness and excitement would rush through my body. I always loved that feeling!

When I was younger and not yet jaded by Society's lies, I

truly believed I could do anything. Those feelings surged through me regularly. For me, goose bumps were the natural response to watching someone overcome a significant obstacle in their life through hard work and sacrifice and ultimately succeed, proving all the skeptics wrong. I remember being covered in goose bumps the first time I watched the original *Rocky*. I am pretty sure I turned into a goose bump when I watched the movie *Rudy* too!

For me, goose bumps are an involuntary response synonymous with following your Path in life—they're a sign of living an Authentic Life. When was the last time you got goose bumps? Do you remember what caused them? What connects with you on such an emotional level that your body secretes enough adrenaline to produce them? Think hard, because this is where your Purpose lies. Lasting success in life comes from following a Path that leads you closer and closer to your Purpose. You're headed in the right direction whenever you get goose bumps!

If you've made it this far in the book, you've spent some time gathering your thoughts on what Freedom means to you. You've developed a rough Vision of what's required for you to live a more autonomous life. You understand it won't be easy to get there. Staying true to who you are and not allowing yourself to follow someone else's rules never is. We are all wired to try and fit in with the tribe. But you picked up this book for a reason, and if you want to find your Freedom, you might as well understand right now that it's going to be a struggle. Getting there will require you to take a much more difficult Path than the one you are currently on.

Along this Path, you'll get winded, frustrated, and maybe even turned around. There will be obstacles so challenging you may consider returning to the comfort of Society's Box. What's more, others won't be able to help with some of the problems you encounter. They've never tried what you're embarking on, and their advice will only serve you so much. To ensure success on your new Path, it's critical to set your Purpose as true north on your compass, rather than your current passion. This is because passions change over time; their flames burn out. Purpose's fire is eternal; it burns from the essence of who you are.

Finding Freedom by following your Purpose gives you the intrinsic motivation to go Against the Grain and stay on the Path. One without the other is like having Waze on your smartphone, but no tower in the area to provide a signal. Don't make the mistake of pursuing Freedom without first determining your Purpose. Let me explain why.

> Going Against the Grain requires a focus on Purpose—not just Freedom.

The battle cry for these people is "Screw the nine to five! I hate my job and my boss. I don't want to answer to anyone but myself!" People who take this approach understand that Freedom grows in their lives when they own a business, rental property, or another type of asset that provides a consistent stream of positive cash flow, without demanding hours and hours of their time. Their thought process is "I can purchase a car wash or laundromat, hire a good manager, and then do what I want during the week for the rest of my life." The most important goal is to be your own boss and call your own shots.

What inevitably happens to the new business owner when he tries breaking out of Society's Box, focusing solely on Freedom? Obstacles arise. Competition opens next door. Technology changes the business model. Key employees quit so they can do their own thing. Margins get skinny, or even evaporate. These obstacles force them to get back into the day-to-day of running the business. If you don't love what your business or service provides to the customer in the first place, the company may fail from your lack of participation.

I've seen it happen too many times. An employee, drowning in Corporate America's embalming fluid, realizes she hates her job and wants to own her own business. While researching companies to own, she listens to entrepreneurial guru after entrepreneurial guru explaining the benefits of owning a car wash or laundromat. Finally, the employee quits her corporate job and purchases a laundromat with her hard-earned savings. But the new business owner never had any genuine interest in running a laundromat. She purchased the business only to provide the monthly cash flow needed to support her new life without a boss.

Two years later, she's facing obstacles that have arisen (they always do), but she has no emotional connection with the business. Margins continue to deteriorate from a lack of new direction. Before you know it, the new business owner is scrambling to sell at a yard sale price or simply has to close the business down and declare bankruptcy. What felt like Freedom turns into a reality worse than having a nine-to-five.

How do you establish this marriage of Freedom with Purpose? It's not easy, but you can do it. After quitting my job as plant manager, it took me a couple of years to figure it out. After nine years of trying to swim in the embalming fluid of Corporate America, three things eventually combined to lead me in the direction of my Purpose.

When Elliot and I initially left our jobs at the Torrington Company, we knew we wanted to own our own company. We took the least costly step we could and started a small consulting company called Islands of Success. Our goal was to help small to midsized manufacturing firms implement world-class manufacturing techniques, which we had already done at the Standard Plant.

We immediately landed our first consulting job with a local sheet metal company purchased by a "downsized" corporate executive who had little experience running a manufacturing facility. The company had tons of problems with schedule attainment due to high defect levels and poor inventory control. We began installing a pull production system on the shop floor with empowered work teams to handle most day-to-day decision-making in the production process. But the plant manager was the grandson of the company's founder, and he didn't value the shop floor workers' input. He refused to turn over the day-to-day control of the manufacturing process to the people doing the work.

I found myself right back in the same situation as my old corporate job, minus the boss. I knew what we needed to do to transform this plant into a money-making machine, filled with inspired workers who enjoyed what they did, but I didn't have the authority to make it happen. Elliot and I landed a second consulting job with another small manufacturing company, and we ran into precisely the same situation. We found another owner who felt the need to control everything, without the courage to empower his workforce and move the company forward. Two years after quitting my corporate job, I knew I would never be happy working for someone else.

I was beating my head against the desk in my home office,

realizing I wasn't any happier on my own than I had been as plant manager. We learned that even small manufacturing companies that were for sale were priced much higher than Elliot and I could afford. I got walloped with the understanding that the world just moved on without you; I never heard from those I thought were close friends in my previous corporate life. I transitioned from old workdays filled with meetings, surrounded by other employees, to spending the majority of my time alone in my home office. I wondered what the hell I had done!

I had no idea how lonely walking Against the Grain could be. How humbling it would be to go from leading hundreds of people to only managing myself. But the yin to loneliness's yang? The time to figure out what truly mattered to me. The time to do things I could only dream about when I was climbing the corporate ladder. Two other factors amplified my frustration with consulting, and they finally led me on the Path toward my Purpose.

My maternal grandmother died of a massive heart attack at the age of 51. My mother inherited her poor genetics in regard to her lipid levels, and had visible cholesterol deposits on her lower eyelids when she was only in her thirties. Mom had them burned off, and it's something I have never forgotten from my childhood. My brother and I began following the same low-fat, low-cholesterol diet my mother was required to follow, along with annual fast-ing blood tests to measure our lipid levels. Due to playing sports year-round and exercising consistently through college, I had always kept my lipid levels in check. But climbing the corporate ladder took my attention away from my health. Twelve-hour days and high stress levels contributed to its overall deterioration.

Upon accepting the plant manager position, I completed a full physical, which was required for upper-level management. The results weren't good. Even though I still looked like I was in shape, I had stopped exercising with any regularity. My blood test results were downright scary. My cholesterol was over 350, and my triglycerides topped 1,400! I immediately went back to my regular doctor to recheck the results, and he confirmed my blood lipids were so high they could see yellowish fat in the vials of blood drawn from my arm.

My doctor told me if I didn't reduce the stress in my life and get back to the good eating and exercise habits I had always adhered to, I would most likely have a heart attack by the time I was 50. I was only 32. I had been genetically unlucky and inherited the same exceedingly high lipid levels of my grandmother and mother. My deteriorating health was the second factor that pushed me toward my Purpose.

My doctor prescribed a statin for cholesterol and another

triglyceride-lowering drug that helped right away. I became a zealot to improve my health. Deep down, I now understand this blood test directly impacted my decision to leave my job as plant manager. The reality check helped me see that the Path I was on was leading me in the wrong direction. After leaving Corporate America, I got myself into the best shape of my life! The gym became my sanctuary. I was obsessed with understanding how the human body utilized nutrition and exercise to improve overall fitness. I went so far as to study and sit for a four-hour exam, and I became a certified personal trainer within the National Strength and Conditioning Association (NSCA).

The final factor that drove me toward my Purpose was my lifelong dream to be a football coach. Shortly after quitting my job as plant manager, I applied for a vacant assistant coaching position with the local high school football team. I needed to fill a hole in my life that had been there since my high school years.

I spent two years coaching the defensive line and wide receivers. I also became the head strength and conditioning coach for the team. While the new consulting gig still left me feeling empty when it came to work, being part of the football team gave me daily inspiration. I had an absolute blast with the other coaches during daily practice and while scouting games. I was slowly coming back to my senses.

When the head coach put me in charge of the weight room, I realized just how much I loved helping others improve their fitness. What was it about going to the gym? The music playing, the weights clanging, people embracing the struggle to improve their health and wellness? I realized I had always loved going to the gym and getting in a good workout. My love affair with exercise started when I was a skinny eight-year-old with a Joe Weider barbell, flat bench, and sand-filled plastic weights. Whenever my parents needed to find me, they only had to walk down the stairs into our basement to find me lifting weights.

There was something intoxicating about pushing past my comfort zone and getting stronger and faster. It made me feel alive. Little did I know, it was to become the metaphor for my life. My love of fitness originated from being smaller than average and feeling the need to prove to anyone who ever said, "You're too small to do that" that they were wrong. I would do whatever it took to be one of the strongest and fastest kids in my class. I was always doing push-ups, sit-ups, pull-ups, and running sprints. I won every physical education test in my grade from elementary through high school.

After years away and focusing on other, less authentic interests, fitness found its way back into my life. Whenever I found myself helping others improve their health, goose bumps covered me! It all culminated one day while eating lunch with Elliot at our favorite local restaurant. Elliot said he had located another small manufacturing company for sale in a nearby town. Without thinking, I blurted out, "I'm no longer interested in manufacturing. I'd like to own a gym."

Think back through your life. What experiences gave you goose bumps as a kid? How about as a teenager? A young adult? Keep moving forward. Look for strands that tie the experiences together. What are you doing when you get goose bumps? What is the little muse sitting on your shoulder trying to tell you? If you hope to succeed in going Against the Grain, the realization of your Purpose must be your destination. Listen closely to that little voice in your head, your Authentic Self, whenever you get goose bumps. Building the second leg of your stool depends on finding your *why*.

Phil Knight, the founder of Nike, wondered why he sucked at selling encyclopedias and mutual funds, but how selling new sneakers somehow came easy to him. In his excellent book, *Shoe Dog*, Phil states,

> Driving back to Portland, I'd puzzle over my sudden success at selling. I'd been unable to sell encyclopedias, and I'd despised it to boot. I'd been slightly better at selling mutual funds, but I'd felt dead inside. So why was selling shoes so different? Because, I'd realized, it wasn't selling. I *believed* in

running. I believed that if people got out and ran a few miles every day, the world would be a better place, and I believed these shoes were better to run in. People, sensing my belief, wanted some of that belief for themselves. Belief, I decided. Belief is irresistible.

Phil didn't start Nike with a clearly defined business plan complete with five years of financial proformas. He just continued to follow an obsession. That obsession was his Purpose. Think of the things you resort to when you have free time. What activities completely engross you? What are you doing when you finally look at your watch and realize you don't know where the time has gone? As Jesse Itzler so expertly stated on the *3-of-7 Podcast* with Chadd Wright, "If you are in your correct, authentic lane in life, your inspiration never runs dry." That authentic lane is your Purpose. I agree with Jesse and his method of trying to find your Purpose. Jesse asks you to answer the following questions:

- What do you love doing that makes you both happy and proud?
- What are you good at? Maybe not great at it now, but you love it to the point that you know you can become great at it. What is it you know you will develop a deep expertise in because you are obsessed with it?
- How can you help others with this current or eventual expertise?

Put them all together, and you've found your Purpose.

Another expert in finding Purpose is Simon Sinek. I highly recommend his excellent book, *Find Your Why*. In it, Simon describes the essential value of a Why Statement. It's a simple statement comprised of two parts. First, it describes the contribution you want to make to the world and the lives of others. Second, it states the impact your contribution will have. My Why Statement for this book is: *to give readers the inspiration and plan to break free from Society's chains so they can live the life they want to live.*

The bottom line is that you'll never find Freedom following someone else's dream. Steven Pressfield asks this best in his book *The War of Art*. He asks, "If you were the last person here on earth, what would you still be doing?" Think about that question; when there is no one left to impress, what would you still be doing? What are you on this earth to do?

Cameron Hanes would still be running and hunting. Jocko Willink would still be getting up at 4:30 a.m. for his daily workout. Would you still be doing your day job if no one else was around? Not for the recognition or the money, but simply because you enjoyed the work of that activity? If the answer is no, you're not being true to your Authentic Self. Whatever you would be doing, regardless of whether or not you were paid, that's where your Purpose lies. *That's where you'll find your goose bumps.* That's what will keep you moving forward, Against the Grain, and toward your Freedom.

If you're stuck trying to get your arms around what drives and energizes your Authentic Self, do something outside of your current comfort levels. Stretch your limits. Register for a challenging obstacle race like a Tough Mudder or Spartan Race. Take an art class or try to learn another language.

Do something that forces you to struggle. In the uncomfortable moments, when we don't have the energy to make excuses for our choices, our true desires and goals become clearer. Much like having a rough outline before you begin writing a book, you need the general realization of what gives you goose bumps to live a more Authentic Life. Use that clarity to create your rough outline. Write down the best Why Statement you can for who you are right now so you have a guiding light as you move forward.

With both your Vision of Freedom and Why Statement down on paper, you've built the first two legs of the stool you need to reach the key hidden on top of the door that opens to your Authentic Life. I wrote this book to help you create the life you want and the autonomy to enjoy it. If you love what you do, you'll find a way to turn every obstacle into an opportunity. The next chapter will explain the stool's final leg, and why it's the most crucial one of all.

CHAPTER 5

IT'S ALL ABOUT THEM

*"A person who lives selfishly will not **go** to hell. They will **live** in hell."*

—RYAN HOLIDAY

It was stifling hot in my grandfather's income-adjusted senior apartment that he shared with my stepgrandmother. I had thankfully remembered to wear a T-shirt under my hoodie, knowing that my little 85-year-old Italian grandfather would still have hands as cold as ice in his 90-degree apartment. As was our custom, Gramps poured me a cold beer and offered me a square of cheddar cheese topped with a slice of pepperoni. I swear he lived on this food combination! I was only a couple of months away from graduating from UCONN, and I stopped by to tell him I had accepted my first real job out of college as an entry-level project engineer for the Torrington Company.

My grandfather took a sip of his beer, looked at me, and said, "Congratulations, grandson. I have no doubt you will be very successful. Let me give you some advice from working for over 30 years on the shop floor at Jacobs Rubber Company. Stay the humble young man you've always been. Don't go into your first job thinking you know more than the worker running the shop floor equipment. No one knows more than the person doing the job. Listen closely to the shop floor workers, treat them with the respect they deserve, and you'll get more accomplished than any of the other engineers who think their degrees make them smarter than everyone else."

Little did I know then, but it was the single best piece of advice I would ever receive about living a successful life.

I have come to understand that if your Purpose doesn't hinge on helping *others* succeed, you don't have a Purpose. You have a goal. True Purpose comes from being of service to others. It's never the other way around.

Chapter 3 asked you to create your Vision of Freedom. Chapter 4 helped you develop your Why Statement, your Purpose. Now it's time to answer the most critical question of all: who are you going to help succeed in life by combining your Vision with your Purpose?

When the reason for breaking out of Society's Box is

your belief that the product or service you provide will help others live a better life, your chances of success rise exponentially. It's realizing the fundamental truth to the saying, "A high tide lifts all boats." You become the tide when your Vision for living an Authentic Life centers on helping others succeed. Society wants us to be self-serving, but our Authentic Selves want to do what's best for the greatest number of people possible.

Think of the "successful" people you know regarding wealth and status, and conversations you may have had with them. If the discussions were honest, you'll remember statements such as, "It's lonely at the top," "Getting here isn't what I thought it would be," and "I don't know who I can trust anymore." Too many people take the Path called Against the Grain with their Vision of Freedom centered on personal wealth: "Once I have enough money, I can do whatever I want." Their Purpose focuses on improving themselves: "I'm going to be famous." They end up wealthy and celebrated with all the autonomy in the world, but with no one else to enjoy their newfound Freedom with. The joke ends up being on them. They've reached a false summit—Society's summit—and find themselves very lonely at the top.

How could this happen?

They never finished building their stool, and they opened

the wrong door. *They're still on Society's Path!* They failed to understand that living an Authentic Life has, at its core, the credo: "It's not about *you*; it's all about *them!*" I took the advice my grandfather gave me very seriously. I became a team player at a very young age. Organized sports consistently drove this point home for me. Being elected co-captain of my high school football team by my teammates was a highlight during my teenage years.

I understood my success as a running back and the local paper write-ups were due to my 10 teammates in the offensive huddle. Alone, I would have gotten nowhere. This knowledge became a part of who I was. It was deeply ingrained in my psyche long before I accepted my first job out of college.

I'll never forget my ritual during the early morning drives to work as a new project engineer at the Standard Plant. I blasted Bon Jovi's "Living on a Prayer" in my new Chevy Beretta, belted out the verses, and felt my body get covered in goose bumps. I listened to the story of Tommy and Gina and thought of the factory workers and the strikes they had previously endured. I thought of the repetitive, routine jobs, and the small hourly pay they received. I committed to keeping that old plant open and giving the workers a meaningful voice in improving their workplace. Success wasn't about me and what I could do to improve the bottom line. My commitment was to create the best work environment for everyone and let everyone impact our success. I remembered the wisdom of my grandfather and put the workers first, especially above what would have been the "right choice" for my career at the time.

When tasked with improving the quality and competitiveness of a new manufacturing cell in the factory, I personally introduced myself to each pump vane cell worker. These workers were spread over three shifts. Many of them reminded me of my grandfather. I looked each of them in the eye and let them know I was merely there to help them fix what they already knew was wrong. I told them the truth: "I may have just graduated from college with an engineering degree, but I know next to nothing when it comes to producing pump vanes. You're the experts. I'm here to listen and learn from you. You can tell me what needs to be changed so it will become easy to produce the highest-quality pump vanes in the world."

My *why* was to improve this product line's performance by setting the goal of continual improvement and seeking the help, input, and support of those doing the work. Success came from getting the people running the equipment to take ownership of the product they were making, its quality, and its future. It was all about them, not about me.

What I learned in this factory became the foundation of my success in business and life. When I eventually purchased my own business, I used my genuine belief in the servant leadership model to create a culture of workforce ownership throughout the organization. It was a culture that didn't accept excuses when we didn't reach our goals; it was a culture where the employees clearly understood what I wanted from them, and were equipped with whatever they needed to succeed. I feel confident that the employees of the various companies I have both worked for and owned knew I greatly appreciated their input and who they were.

Every business leader or business owner's primary goal should be to help their employees succeed. It should never be the other way around. Every time I find a poorly performing business, the owner is in it for themselves. Every time I see a poorly performing life, the same truth holds. The person continues to look at life with a "What's in it for me?" attitude. I've never thought that way.

There was nothing better than seeing an entry-level employee with a great work ethic put their nose to the grindstone, do more than was expected of the job, and get promoted. So many of my Torrington Company, World Gym, Planet Fitness, and Blitz Indoor Trampoline Park team members eventually left my employment and successfully landed the jobs they wanted in life. I supported their growth every step of the way. Nothing makes me happier than the relationships I continue to have with them to this day.

The following is a list of many of the outstanding people I have employed throughout my varied career. For those I may have missed, I apologize. I hope you know how much each of you has inspired me through our many years of friendship.

Nelson: project engineer to Wall Street bond trader to cryptocurrency trader

Scott: project engineer to superintendent to director of manufacturing

Gabe: personal trainer to medical equipment sales director

Danah: front desk employee to club manager to real estate broker

Ken: personal trainer to head strength and conditioning coach for a professional hockey team

Mark: front desk supervisor to collegiate head strength and conditioning coach

Lori: club manager to area partner of a fast-growing boutique fitness franchise

Sarah: club manager to Coca-Cola district sales manager and gym owner with her husband

James: front desk employee to regional manager and youth pastor for his church

Sam: front desk employee to assistant manager to full-time policeman

Matt: front desk employee to assistant manager to full-time Army Reserve and helicopter crew chief

Mark: business partner at Blitz Indoor Trampoline Park to owner of multiple muffler repair shops

Helping others should be the foundation of your Purpose. If you desire more Freedom in your own life, help others find the same. Your effort creates the positive energy to sustain everyone's march forward. My belief is a simple one:

The function of Freedom is to free someone else.

My focus on helping others find their authentic Paths started with the shop floor workers in an old wooden floor factory. It continued with my employees at my gym, and expanded to include my new business partner and our employees at Blitz Indoor Trampoline Park. It was a damn good 20-year run.

Then life threw one of its proverbial curveballs.

My family had moved to New Hampshire to help open Blitz Indoor Trampoline Park and rented a home until we had a better idea of how things would turn out. We still owned our townhouse and Planet Fitness in Connecticut. During one of my biweekly visits to the gym, I walked into my office and found a certified letter on my desk. Per my signed franchise agreement, the letter stated that my franchisor had decided my gym would have to be moved to a better retail location and expand from 12,000 to 20,000 square feet to meet the current franchise agreement requirements. The move and expansion would cost me close to $2 million. Failure to move and expand my location would result in the nonrenewal of my franchise agreement, which expired in a year.

What was I going to do? My family had fallen in love with New Hampshire. We lived fifteen minutes from the beach, only an hour from Boston, and two hours from the White Mountains. It was time to make a critical long-term decision. Should we stay in New Hampshire and look for additional locations to open more trampoline parks? Or move back to Connecticut and relocate the gym?

It was time to be brutally honest with myself. I had ignored my philosophy when I had accepted sweat equity in the indoor trampoline park. While I thoroughly enjoyed helping my new business partner (a first-time business owner) and our young managers learn the basics of running a successful company, a packed house of screaming kids didn't give me goose bumps. If my family wanted to stay in New Hampshire, I didn't want to continue operating indoor trampoline parks.

Possibilities overwhelmed my brain. Should we move back to Connecticut? Relocate the gym? Sell my ownership interest in the trampoline park and the gym in Connecticut, and start a different New Hampshire business? The sleepless nights began. My love has always been fitness, and we researched many new boutique franchise offerings. We spent months combing through franchise disclosure documents (FDDs) and meeting with regional developers. Then, I got punched in the gut. My franchisor handcuffed me with a two-year noncompete if I sold the gym, which prevented me from doing anything that involved fitness. I was standing at a crossroads. What the hell was I going to do?

The lightbulb finally flickered during a weeklong vacation at a friend's beach house. I woke up one morning, grabbed a hot cup of coffee from the Keurig, and took a seat on the outdoor balcony overlooking the beach below. It was early in the morning, and the only sound was the waves crashing rhythmically against the shore. I was struggling to determine what to do next. I was desperately trying to figure what was next for me and was focused solely on myself. I had completely lost sight of the real goal—*helping others find Freedom.*

Clarity came in an instant.

My thoughts immediately shifted to my wife, Stephanie. She was my biggest supporter. She had sold her three-room massage therapy business back in Connecticut to move to New Hampshire and help open Blitz. She'd recently gone back to work for a local massage therapy business to help provide extra household income. After years of owning her own business, I knew she was miserable being an employee again.

When she woke up, I told her to have a seat next to me on the balcony. I couldn't wipe the grin off my face. I asked,

"Instead of focusing on what I want to do next if I sell the gym, what if we focus on what *you* want to do for the next 10 years? It's your turn to enjoy the type of Freedom I've had from owning the gym." The smile that came across her face gave me goose bumps. It was time to focus on helping my best friend find the Freedom I had experienced over the last 18 years.

We immediately contacted a franchise consultant who lived in our area of New Hampshire. During our initial phone conversation, Stephanie asked, "What franchise could New Hampshire use that isn't here yet, and fits with my massage therapy background and Craig's love of helping others succeed in business?" Within seconds, our franchise consultant said, "This may sound a little crazy, but I think the perfect next franchise for the two of you is Sola Salon Studios!" I can remember my wife's startled look as we shot glances at each other, and both said in unison, "A hair salon?"

We learned during our franchise discovery call with Sola Corporate that the overriding goal of the franchise model was "to inspire and support beauty professionals to chase their dreams, elevate their careers, and experience the Freedom of salon ownership."

The business model involves renting commercial space and building out 20 to 40 fully furnished boutique studios for established stylists, barbers, aestheticians, massage therapists, and other beauty and health professionals. Each studio comes complete with cabinetry, shampoo bowls, chairs, mirrors, and a soundproof sliding glass door.

The founders created Sola Salon Studios to help beauty and health professionals transition to business ownership without the traditional risk and expense of signing a five- to 10-year commercial lease on top of spending lots of money for a buildout. A beauty or health professional simply pays weekly rent to own their boutique salon! They can decorate the studio as they see fit, have 24/7 access to it, carry whatever products they want, and keep all profits! Steph and I got goose bumps!

Steph would be able to open her own massage therapy business within our Sola, and we would be helping motivated professionals experience the Freedom of business ownership. We flew out to Sola headquarters in Denver and fell in love with the franchise team. We bought franchising rights in New Hampshire with the proceeds from my ownership interest in Blitz. We decided to sell the gym in Connecticut and use the sale proceeds to start this new franchise opportunity in New Hampshire.

It was time to turn our lives upside down again! The struggle and joy of opening a new business began. It took over a year to find a suitable location for our Sola. We finally found a spot in Portsmouth, and we opened with 40 percent of the studios preleased. My wife leased one of the studios for herself and opened her new massage therapy business, Unravel Therapeutic Massage! Within six months of opening, our first Sola location was 100 percent occupied with a waiting list!

It's time to be honest. I struggled greatly. Selling my gym and accepting a new role within our family supporting my wife while she worked tirelessly to get Sola Portsmouth leased and Unravel Therapeutic Massage up and running has been humbling. Not having employees to lead at Blitz or Planet Fitness left me struggling for a sense of personal Purpose once again. Embracing the belief that "it's all about them" can be very tricky at times. Your damn ego keeps trying to take control while whispering in your ear, "What about you? You're the guy doing all the work behind the scenes. You're the guy who came up with the idea in the first place. You need to get the credit for what's happening here!"

There were countless days I struggled with my ego after doing the weekly grocery shopping, getting the laundry done and put away, working on this book and my consulting jobs, and having dinner ready when my wife got home from a long day of work. I constantly worried what our new friends in New Hampshire thought when I was the parent dropping off and picking up our daughter at school. So, I focused on the daily work I needed to do. I got up early, exercised, made breakfast for Brenna, and got her off to school. I made sure that when Steph finally got home from Sola each evening, she had some time to relax.

After writing this book and doing a lot of self-reflection, I realize the kryptonite to ego is love. Simply love. My love for Stephanie was stronger than my need for affirmation. And the look on her face as the construction came together and she signed her first couple of leases made the struggle worth it. Helping someone else succeed always is! It's a lesson I learned from a very wise and happy grandfather, and I hope I have impressed it upon you.

If your reason for going Against the Grain centers on *you*, you will end up disappointed. More money for you. A fancier car for you. A bigger house for you. More status for you. If you work hard enough, you may get everything you're striving for and end up feeling empty in the process. Please listen to what I am trying to tell you. *Don't focus on yourself.* Instead, focus on improving the lives of those you are responsible for, and your life will improve, as well.

If you are a manager, focus on helping your employees succeed rather than sucking up to the boss, hoping for the next promotion. If you are a parent, make sure your children understand success in life happens when they can't tell the difference between work and pleasure. Help them live authentically. If you are a business owner, help your employees succeed by teaching them what it takes to run a successful enterprise. Success on the Path of your Authentic Self depends on your ability to create trust with others. Trust is established by eliminating your ego and putting others first. *Trust is the foundation of everything good in life.*

We've come to a critical juncture in your quest to break out of Society's Box. You have a clear Vision of what Freedom means to you. You have a Purpose, and it's focused on helping others succeed. Congratulations! You've built the three legs of the stool you need to reach the key and unlock the door to your Authentic Life. You're standing in front of the door you've always dreamed of opening. What's that pit you suddenly feel in your stomach?

Why are you hesitating to unlock the damn door?!

CHAPTER 6

YOU MUST BECOME FRIENDS WITH FEAR

"At the root of every emotion holding us back, we will often find a hidden fear. It is no surprise, then, that the number one reason why people say they are not living the life they want is fear."

—AKSHAY NANAVATI

It was a typical New England winter morning, cold enough that as I walked from my car into the gym, the snow squeaked under my boots. I had owned World Gym of Enfield for just over a year, and I had recently purchased some new strength training equipment. The members loved it. We were coming into the busy season, and I was happy to see our membership growing, slowly but surely. As I sat down at the desk in my office, I heard one of my front counter employees greet my landlord's wife and tell her I was in the office. I looked up from the desk as she walked to my office entrance with a concerned look on her face. She had something in her hand. She looked at me sternly and said, "The rent check bounced. What's going on here?"

I suddenly felt like I was floating outside of my body and looking down at this scene from above. Was I dying? If so, why wasn't I seeing the warm, calming light everyone else talked about during near-death experiences? I snapped out of it, took the check from her hand, apologized, and said my accountant must have been playing the float in the checking account too closely. I assured her there was plenty of money in our savings account to pay the rent, and I would have Elliot, my accountant, transfer the funds and rewrite the check when he came in. She thanked me and left the gym.

I tried to call Elliot and only got his voicemail. I left him an angry message explaining what had just happened and that the rent needed to get paid first thing the next day. It was odd I didn't hear back from him, but I knew Elliot was busy working on other things. He had accepted a full-time job when I purchased the gym. He usually stopped by early in the morning to pay the bills and get the office accounting done before traveling to his real job.

I went into the gym earlier than usual the next day, hoping

to catch Elliot. My front counter employee told me he came in quickly, closed the office door, and left without saying goodbye. My heart sank again. I walked into the office and found a sealed envelope addressed to me lying on his desk. I opened the letter and read Elliot's handwritten note stating he was in over his head with his new full-time job and helping me with the gym. He was walking away from the gym, and he asked that I please let him go. The letter stated I could keep the money he let me borrow—it was the least he could do as my friend.

I was in shock. My level of fear had never been higher. I had left all the accounting and office management responsibilities entirely with Elliot. Hell, I didn't even know how to use QuickBooks! But I did know we always kept a handwritten balance sheet for the gym's operating checkbook, and I scurried around looking for the little white binder. When I found it, I realized Elliot hadn't balanced it in over a month! I found the paid invoice folder and manually balanced the operating bank account. The business checking account balance was just over $20,000 in the red after paying the rent! My heart rate reached its max.

The business checking account had been in the red for months. Elliot was using the "float" at the bank to cover the invoices, but got caught when the landlord cashed a rent check on time. What the hell was I going to do? When I looked in the open invoice folder, I nearly had a stroke.

I found past due notices from both our health insurance company and our power company. Both accounts were scheduled for termination in 14 days if there was no receipt of payments due.

My mind was racing. How the hell did this happen?

Toward the end of my first year owning the gym, I knew we needed to reinvest and give the members something new to build excitement with the recent ownership change. I proposed spending $15,000 for a new line of plate-loaded resistance training equipment. Elliot disagreed and argued we hadn't yet made the profits to reinvest. "You have to save the money before you can spend it, Craig," were his exact words.

We were coming into the busy season for a gym, and I wanted to give the members something to tell their friends about to drive new memberships. With only a tiny marketing budget, we needed more referrals to grow our membership base. In my heart, I knew the new equipment would be the start of the momentum we needed to do just that. I listened to my gut, ordered the plate-loaded equipment, and drained our operating account. Luckily, the purchase produced precisely the response I had hoped for among the members. They were excited to see something new at the gym, told their friends about it, and our membership base started to grow!

I didn't understand the $15,000 spent on the equipment was needed to pay the bills and keep the gym doors open. Elliot had done his best to keep the gym open by playing the bank float with invoice payments, but the equipment purchase left no cash to float. We were caught with our pants down. It was terrifying.

Moments of terror and panic seemed to be a constant in my life. I grew up on a steady diet of fear. It began as a young child, fearing not living up to the expectations of a very demanding father. The fear of not having all my father's projects done perfectly and on time. I'll be the first to admit, it wasn't a fun way to grow up, but I realize now that fear drove me to accomplish much more than I would have without it. Each time I overcame my fear and completed the tasks set before me, my self-confidence grew.

I remember my fear of playing team sports when I was young. The fear of asking the prettiest girl at school out on a date. The fear of walking onto the UCONN football team. The fear of starting my first real job at the Torrington Company, and leading the charge of changing a century-old unionized manufacturing plant's culture. The fear of accepting the position of plant manager with the livelihoods of over 500 people at stake. The fear of quitting that job and starting a consulting company. The fear of cashing in my 401(k) to purchase a failing World Gym.

I learned an important lesson early in my life:

Each time my life improved, the first step was always toward my fear.

Only now do I understand the connection between my Path Against the Grain and the importance of facing my fears. The two are welded together. The foundation for going Against the Grain is self-confidence. Self-confidence is developed by overcoming your fears. I overcame my worries by realizing how badly I always wanted what was on the other side of fear. Every victory over fear resulted from an obsession with doing something I hadn't done before.

But when I finished reading Elliot's letter, the fear came rushing back.

This time it was the fear of going bankrupt and being broke in my early thirties. It was the fear of failing at my first attempt to own a business after quitting my high-paying, high-status corporate job. All I could hear in my head were the voices of everyone who had told me it was crazy to quit my job! Once again, what I initially thought was fear was my ego trying to steer me back onto the safe and comfortable Path. I already knew that going out of business was a real option on the table for every young entrepreneur. Once again, I laughed to myself and told my ego to go back to bed. My love for this gym overcame my fear of looking like a failure. Only when you genuinely love what you are doing, along with the people you are doing it with, will you stay committed to your Authentic Self.

I drove out to Elliot's home, sat on his porch with him, and tried to figure out what was going on. Elliot explained he had been trying to manage the cash flow with the bank float and apologized for not telling me how bad it had gotten. He didn't want me worrying about the finances; he wanted me to stay focused on growing the membership base for the gym to survive. Elliot agreed to come back to the gym and help until he documented everything he did in the office and I could take over those duties.

I asked Elliot if I could borrow more money, as I had none left. He quickly stated it made no sense to put more good money into a potentially failing business. The money he had let me borrow was mine, but he wasn't going to loan me any more. He no longer felt confident the gym was going to survive. I now had a much bigger problem to solve. I needed to fund $20,000 in the operating account to pay the rent, utilities, and medical insurance!

No bank was going to loan me money. My bank had already turned down my application for a line of credit, but I could keep the business alive a little longer by maxing out my credit cards. I could ask my parents if they'd loan me the money to help keep my gym alive. But how was I going to ask my father? He was the guy who, only a year ago, loved to take me out to breakfast with his buddies and brag about my plant manager title and how much money I made. He was the guy who looked me in the face when I bought the gym and said, "You are an engineer with an MBA, and you're buying a damn gym. You had a great job as a plant manager, and you were making more money than I ever came close to making in my entire life. I hope you know what you are doing, because I think this is a piss-poor decision."

I wasn't willing to give up on my dream. I finally owned my own business! I knew the improvement plan I had created for the gym was working. Slowly, but it was still working. More people were signing up each month than were canceling, and the members' attitudes were more positive. I looked fear in the face again, bit the bullet, and asked my parents if I could borrow $35,000. I would use $20,000 to bring the checkbook back to a slightly positive balance, and $15,000 to replace what I spent on the new equipment.

Asking them was the hardest thing I had ever done in my life.

My father immediately rejected my request and told me to ask Elliot for more money. If Elliot was so supportive of my decision to leave my corporate job and purchase this gym, then he should help! I explained to my father that Elliot had already turned down my request, and the bank had turned down my application for a line of credit. He was my last resort. There was a long period of silence on the phone. My father told me he would speak to my mother and get back to me the following day. I reminded him my power would be turned off next week. It was a sleepless night.

My mother called me the next day and told me that, of course, they would let me borrow the $35,000. She would drive the check out later in the day so I could deposit it into the bank and pay the past due bills. My father wanted to treat it like a bank loan with required monthly payments and interest, but I explained to him I couldn't do that. We had to be cash flow positive and have extra cash before I could start paying the loan back. I promised him I would purchase nothing personally until I repaid them in full.

I kept my promise.

The rest is history. Over the next couple of years, I paid my parents back in full (with interest). Overcoming my fear and borrowing $35,000 from my parents resulted in my owning the gym for 18 years and creating an incredible life filled with autonomy.

As you stand in front of the locked door that opens to your Authentic Life, the pit you feel in your stomach is *fear*. *Fear* is stopping you from unlocking the door!

By its very nature, going Against the Grain brings you face-to-face with your biggest fears: fear of judgment, fear of failure, and even fear of success. I've learned through real-life experience the only way to get past your fears is to go through them. *You must do what scares you.* You can do it in small baby steps or one giant step, like ripping off a Band-Aid, but until you face your fears and move past them, you will never live an Authentic Life. Instead of letting a racing heart, dry mouth, and stomach full of butterflies stop you from moving forward, set those feelings as the north star on your compass! Create the following mantra and speak it often to yourself:

"When I feel fear, it's just excitement and proof I'm going in the right direction."

Becoming friends with fear is the **Third Guiding Principle** to finding your Freedom and living authentically. I had a racing heart, dry mouth, and a stomach full of butterflies before asking the prettiest girl in my class to be my girlfriend. It's how I felt before every football game, and on the starting line of every motocross race. It's how I felt when I asked Stephanie for her hand in marriage and during the birth of Brenna. For some evolutionary reason, nature programmed humans to despise this physiological response. For most of us, these feelings elicit a compelling voice in our head that screams, "Stop what you are doing! You are going to get hurt!"

Yes, we may get hurt, both physically and emotionally. We may get rejected by the boy or girl. We may get hurt playing the game or competing in the race. We may get rejected by our friends and family for trying to follow a different Path. But what's the alternative? To stay on the sidelines of life with everyone else who is too afraid to face their fears?

The sad truth is, this is how most of us live our lives.

The moment right before we ask a tough question or enter a competition, we often turn the sense of excitement into a false sense of fear. We have a fear of rejection or losing. But it's not real fear. Real fear is when your life is on the line. Fear shouldn't be the outcome of getting turned down in a relationship or failing in some of your endeavors. If you let the possibility of failure create paralyzing fear inside you, you'll eventually spin a thick cocoon around your life that tries to prevent you from ever trying. You'll find yourself tucked neatly inside Society's Box, where you'll do what someone else tells you to do for the rest of your life. If you cannot face your fears, you'll never unlock the door to your Authentic Life. *That's a guarantee.*

Building a habit of moving forward despite my fears throughout my childhood and young adult years was critical to developing the self-confidence I needed to embrace the things that brought excitement into my life. I've seen family members and friends faced with the same decisions I've had to make become frozen by fear and the potential judgment of others. I've seen the goose bumps on their arms and heard the passion in their voices when they explained the new Path they wanted to take. But year after year, they keep coming up with excuses for not taking the next step toward their dream. Don't be one of those people.

Understand that fear never goes away. Ever. Even after borrowing $35,000 from my parents and growing the gym's membership base to generate a good profit, Gold's Gym opened a second location in town only a mile down the road from me. Gold's started offering full gym memberships for only $29.99 per month. I was charging $44 per month. Faster than I could have imagined, 25 percent of my members left for the new gym. My gym dipped back into the red. Fear came rushing back into my life. She had become my regular dance partner.

As luck would have it, my friends Michael and Marc had just started franchising their new low-priced gym concept called Planet Fitness in nearby New Hampshire. Michael called me and said they were offering memberships for as low as $10 per month, and their membership was growing like wildfire! *Ten* dollars per month? It sounded absurd. Was it worth taking the risk of converting my World Gym to a Planet Fitness? I called Michael and spoke with him many times. The familiar sleepless nights came back. I thought back to when I found the courage to quit my plant manager job and build a career around the thing that gave me goose bumps: fitness.

I owned a gym. I was helping hundreds of members improve their lives by improving their health and fitness. If changing the name of my gym from World Gym to Planet Fitness would keep me in the game, I was all in. Finally, I looked in the mirror and said, "What do you have to lose?" I was living an Authentic Life, and I wasn't about to give up on my dream. In one fell swoop, we would become the low-cost fitness center in our community. It was a difficult decision, but it made a lot of sense.

So, I did it.

That single move allowed me to jump from 1,000 members paying an average of $39 a month to 5,000 members paying an average of $14 a month. This gave me an excellent income for the next 15 years! Planet Fitness grew to become one of the largest fitness brands in the country. The cycle of fear that leads to growth never ends if your goal is to live an Authentic Life. Without fear, there is no growth.

Even in my fifties, deciding to write this book caused a lot of fear in me. Attending Scribe's intensive two-day book writing seminar in Austin, Texas, released the same old swarm of butterflies to find a home in my belly. I found it hard to sleep a couple of days before making the trip from New Hampshire to Texas. Who was I to think I could write a book? I was an engineer with an MBA, not an English major.

My fear had won the internal battle for years, always telling me, "You don't need to write a book! You're living a great life and have nothing left to prove." But I felt many readers could benefit from my hard-earned knowledge, and decided to drown out the fear. I booked the trip. I remember the shakiness in my voice when it was my turn to speak in front of the other aspiring Scribe authors about this book and who I was writing it for. It was a stressful couple of days in Texas, but once again, more doors were opened to autonomy.

Even when you understand that fear is an integral part of breaking out of Society's Box and living an Authentic Life, it doesn't make it any easier. Facing your fears is a habit you need to create. If you want to lose weight and get in better shape, you need to adopt regular exercise and eat real food. If you wish to go Against the Grain and live an autonomous life, you need to move toward your fears. The minute you stop experiencing some level of fear in your life, you need to understand you've stopped growing.

Whenever you catch yourself saying, "I would love to try something new in my life right now, but my current job or relationship makes it impossible," you've decided to stay in your comfort zone and not to grow as a person. Growing as a person is scary. It comes with a bucket full of fear. Please don't give in to your worries. Don't continue to listen to Society's lies and stay a slave to someone else's wants and desires.

Make the shift in your mind to rename fear to excitement! Believe with all your soul that a racing heart, dry mouth, and a stomach full of butterflies is a higher power showing you the Path to personal growth. Learn to smile when these feelings invade your brain. There is such a wonderful life on the other side of fear, and doors will open everywhere when you learn to embrace it.

You've built the stool you need to reach the key hidden above the door that leads to your Authentic Life. Your fear is the platform the three legs are attached to. Step on your FEAR, grab the key, and unlock the door!

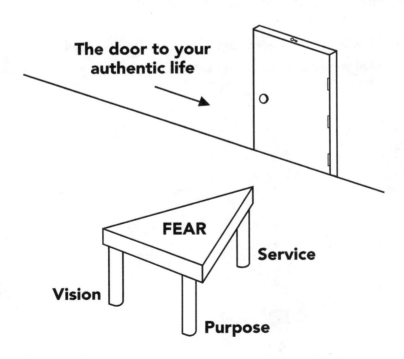

I've got a little homework for you before moving on to the next chapter. Please listen to the song "Fear Is a Liar" by Zach Williams. Listen to it enough times to memorize the words. Here's what everyone's biggest fear in life should be:

Wake up. Eat breakfast. Drive to work in nine-to-five traffic. Work hard all day building someone else's business. Drive home in nine-to-five traffic. Watch TV until you fall asleep. Count down the days until the weekend. Repeat for 40 years.

Once you become friends with fear, you'll be emotionally prepared to go Against the Grain. You can finally unlock the door leading to your Authentic Life.

Now it's time to get yourself financially prepared to survive your climb up the mountain.

———

CHAPTER 7

ARE YOU WILLING TO LIVE BENEATH YOUR MEANS?

"People who live far beneath their means enjoy a freedom that people busy upgrading their lifestyles can't fathom."

—NAVAL RAVIKANT

I had been working at the Torrington Company for just over a year. I lived in a small efficiency apartment at Burlington Arms in Bristol, Connecticut, and made the 20-minute commute each day to work. I had picked this location as my first home away from home because Mike, my best friend and college roommate, lived and grew up in Bristol. Mike took an engineering job with Sikorsky Aircraft and was living with his parents to save some money during his first year. Our goal was to work during the day and meet up after work at The Body Shop, a local gym in Bristol. Friday and Saturday nights were reserved for barhopping and chasing girls. It was a fun way to introduce ourselves to the real world. We celebrated finishing college and landing good jobs by purchasing brand new cars. I bought a Chevy Berreta GT; Mike got a Chevy Camaro Z28. Life was good.

Except for the balance in my bank account.

Something was wrong. I was a new engineer with a higher starting salary than many other nonengineer college graduates. But only a year into my first job, my checking account was hovering near empty. I became friends with Elliot, the chief cost accountant at the Torrington Company. I asked if he could stop by sometime and help me with the large draining sound I heard every time I opened my checkbook. He laughed and offered to come by on a weekend morning to see what he could find.

One Saturday morning, Elliot stopped by my apartment, pulled out his ledger pad, and began organizing my life into a monthly statement of cash flows. It was a straightforward analysis that UCONN must have forgotten to teach their students. Elliot documented the money coming into my household each month versus how much was going out. After combing through my checkbook register and asking a bunch of questions, Elliot put his ledger sheets down along with his number-two pencil, leaned back into the cheap couch I'd found at a yard sale, and gave me that smile all accountants have perfected after they have peered into your soul.

"You've got a cash flow problem, Craig. There's more cash going out of your household each month than there is coming in. It's time to make a hard choice. Turn in your brand-new, 100 percent financed Chevy Beretta, and find a used car you can purchase outright. Or, find an apartment closer to work, and you can split the expense with a roommate. You can't afford the new car payment and the rent for this apartment. There is no money left over for the weekends and having fun. Your savings will be gone within the next six months if you don't make a change. You must learn to live beneath your means, or you'll end up like the majority of my tax clients who live paycheck to paycheck and feel trapped in jobs they despise."

Elliot told me about his tax client who worked at ESPN and made over a million dollars a year, but still lived paycheck to paycheck. Elliot looked me in the eye and declared, "If this guy suddenly lost his job, his family would be out of money in less than a month!" Elliot revealed that many of his clients were in a constant war of "keeping up with the Joneses." They felt the need to have the most prominent homes, expensive cars, and exclusive golf course memberships. These individuals were prisoners within Society's

Box. I had no idea I was learning such an important life lesson early on in my working career.

The following week, I started searching for apartments to rent closer to the factory. As luck would have it, an employee in the pump vane department was looking to rent the first floor of his two-story home, which was only a mile away from the factory. It was a two-bedroom apartment where I could split the rent with a roommate! I had just become the mentor for Tony, a new engineer just hired out of the University of Rhode Island. When I asked if he was interested in moving closer to the factory and splitting the rent with me, he jumped at the chance! We would split an all-inclusive rent of $380 per month!

My rent went from $550 per month plus utilities to $190 per month, all in. I was back to cash flow positive, maxing out my company-matched 401(k), and watching my savings account grow month by month for the first time since purchasing my new car. Elliot taught me a crucial lesson that would play a critical role in finding my Freedom. Financial Freedom isn't about making *more* money. Financial Freedom is about spending *less* money than you make, living beneath your means. It's a hard lesson to learn in our consumption-based lives. People get trapped in Society's Box for financial reasons more than any other. An example that has stayed with me forever happened years after I learned this critical lesson.

I had recently become the Standard Plant manager, and my boss called me into his office. Once I was seated, my boss explained I needed to shut down all start operations immediately. I was dumbfounded. Our team at the plant was doing everything we could to improve the aircraft product line throughput. But we were receiving angry phone calls daily from customers with planes grounded, waiting for our past-due bearings!

I remember looking at my boss in astonishment and saying, "Are you serious? We are getting daily irate calls from customers demanding we expedite their parts, and you are telling me to leave those production orders sitting at start operations?" His answer reveals what happens when you believe Society's lies and get trapped in Society's Box.

"Craig, performance bonuses this year are based on the levels of finished goods inventory held in our factories. The smaller the inventory, the bigger the bonuses. To take this recent promotion to operations manager, I had to leave my plant manager job in Georgia and convince my wife to move our family north to Connecticut. The house I purchased in Connecticut cost more than double what I sold my house for down South. I need my bonus to help pay my mortgage. I'm sorry, but you need to shut off your start operations at the plant so we don't add to our finished goods inventory between now and the end of the year."

This is what happens when you buy into Society's lies. The more money you make, the more things you can purchase. The more things you buy, the higher up the social ladder you can climb. But none of it will lead to the Freedom you desire. Stop believing the lies. It's a trap. You must learn this fact as early in life as possible. Welcome to the **Fourth Guiding Principle** for living an autonomous life: if you spend more than you make, you'll never find Freedom.

A critical step toward finding your Freedom is determining what it will take financially to get you there. For many, going Against the Grain and breaking out of Society's Box means leaving your regular job and a steady paycheck, and starting over with significantly less income. Please listen to this point closely: taking the Path Against the Grain is almost always associated with scaling back your living expenses.

The amount you are willing to scale back and sacrifice financially in the short term will reveal just how committed you are to finding autonomy in the long term. The deeper into Society's lies you bury yourself, the harder it is to dig yourself out. I would love for this message to reach everyone before they decide which college they want to attend or accept their first real job. But whenever you receive this message, it's essential to start making better financial choices as soon as possible. Living beneath your means creates the trap door to breaking out of Society's Box when the time is right.

Understand that the transition from one job to a more fulfilling one or self-employment is never easy financially. The financial sacrifice is probably the number one reason why many people stay stuck in an unfulfilling life. It's scary not to have a steady income. It's even more terrifying if you have a spouse and family to consider. Clearly understanding your monthly budget is critical to your long-term success. Living beneath your means provides a substantial head start to anyone going Against the Grain.

The following is an example of the monthly household operating budget I've used throughout my life. It only measures cash flow—cash in and cash out of your personal or family household. It helps to keep things simple. Include too many details, and it becomes a chore that makes going Against the Grain intolerable. Most of your energy should be put toward the details of living your Purpose, not balancing books.

To figure out your monthly cash flow, first list all the sources of income at the top, and remember to multiply your weekly after-tax income by 4.33 to estimate your monthly total. Next, go through your checkbook register or online banking for the most recent 12-month period, and total all your expenses for the year by type. Do this for all the line items in your household budget and get the annual expenditure of each item. Then, divide the totals by 12 to get an accurate monthly cost for each. Take the time to do the work accurately. This exercise is an excellent learning experience for most people.

Revenue (Net)

Craig: consulting	=	$
Craig: other	=	$
Steph: UPS	=	$
Steph: Unravel Massage	=	$
Craig and Steph: Sola Draw	=	$
TOTAL MONTHLY REVENUE	=	**$XX,XXX (net, after taxes)**

Expenses

Mortgage (including prop. tax)	=	$
Craig: retirement	=	$
Steph: retirement	=	$
Brenna: college savings	=	$
Craig: consulting expenses	=	$
Steph: expenses at Unravel	=	$
Family: Brenna lessons	=	$
Federal and state taxes	=	$
Medical insurance	=	$
Medical co-pays	=	$
Prescription co-pays	=	$
Landscape (lawn and plow)	=	$
Utilities (propane and elect)	=	$
Cable and internet	=	$
Telephone/cell phone	=	$
Homeowners insurance	=	$
Life insurance	=	$
Car and snowmobile insurance	=	$
Miscellaneous/cash	=	$
Credit card payments (food/gas)	=	$
TOTAL MONTHLY EXPENSES	=	**$XX,XXX**
NET INCOME	=	**$XX,XXX (per month)**

For most people, the most significant variable in monthly expenses is credit cards. They are the wildcard that can quickly sink the budget. Dave Ramsey would say to cut up the credit cards, and I understand entirely. Instead, I added extra control and created another simple spreadsheet that records each credit card's weekly balance.

Credit Card Tracking
Personal and Business (closing day)

	(Personal)	AMEX (29th) Personal (CP)	CITI (29th) Personal (SP)	BOA (29th) Personal (CP)	TOTAL DUE
Date:	Due prev. month:	1,041.38	978.41	374.44	**2,394.23**
	as of 06-11-20XX	450.65	374.51	85.16	910.32

	(Business)	AMEX Blue (19th) BEP-Sola (CP)	Capital One (17th) BEP-Sola (CP & SP)	TD Business (3rd) Unravel (SP)	TOTAL DUE
Date:	Due prev. month:	111.46	659.97		**771.43** Sola
				303.88	303.88 Unravel
	as of 06-11-20XX	91.94	578.52		670.46 Sola
				139.99	**139.99 Unravel**

Every Saturday morning, I sit at my laptop and do two things. I balance all checking accounts online, and I log into each personal and business credit card and document its current balance. As you can see from the monthly operating budget, the credit cards have a monthly budget, and the weekly status update allows everyone in the family to see current spending. One week into the month, the expectation is to have used 25 percent of the credit card budget. If you're two weeks into a month and the credit cards have already reached 75 percent of their budget, it's time to cut back on spending. This is a simple tool to keep expenditures within limits.

Establish weekly meetings with your family to review the household budget. Talk about excessive spending and adjust line items if you know things may change in the coming weeks. Use these simple tools to understand your finances clearly and avoid being blindsided by shrinking savings without knowing why.

Once you've adopted a simple budgeting process and have a clear view of your household finances, you can plan for what may happen if you left your job to do something else. You'll learn how much you need to cover the bare essentials while following a new Path in your life. You can preplan for any shortfall during the transition and save a buffer amount to offset any lost income. Remember this—there is always a tremendous amount of stress when changing the direction of your life. Breaking out of Society's Box almost always requires scaling back your life financially. Make sure everyone understands this up front, or it can lead to severe problems.

It eventually did for me.

I used this budgeting process when I decided to leave the Torrington Company and go Against the Grain. I was giving up a large salary, and Elliot and I had no idea how quickly we would land our first client. We created Islands of Success, our management consulting company, while we were still employed, and we started looking for our first client while working out our notices. My monthly household budget was over $1,500 in the red until we landed our first client. Gina and I saved $24,000 to cover the shortfall. Elliot and I landed our first client only a month after leaving the company. But Gina and I were prepared to use all of the $24,000 if we needed to. The monthly household budgeting process has played an integral role every time I've changed paths in life.

We went back to the budget two years into my new consulting career. I was as disappointed with consulting as I was in Corporate America. I desperately wanted to be the owner of my own business! Driven by my frustration, I decided to purchase a failing World Gym a little over an hour away from our home. However, buying the gym required much more drastic cuts to our spending in the short term if we were going to survive financially. Not only would I not get paid until the gym's membership grew enough to pay me, but the purchase also required cashing out my entire 401(k) and taking the penalty for withdrawing at such a young age. Financially, this wasn't the wisest decision, but I was obsessed with owning my own business.

We did our best to live off my wife's income as a morning cook at a convalescent home. There was enough profit at the gym to pay me $1,000 per month to help with the household expenses. Gina and I bought cots and slept in the group exercise room on Friday and Saturday nights to cut travel expenses. It also allowed us to close the gym late on Friday nights and be there to open on weekend mornings. There wasn't any profit to hire more help.

We had to do everything. We cleaned, answered the phone, and gave the tours. We covered as many hours as physically possible. The gym was open from 5:00 a.m. to 10:00 p.m. Monday through Friday, and 8:00 a.m. to 5:00 p.m. Saturday and Sunday. In reality, I lived at the gym seven days a week. Even then, we continued to eat into the small amount of personal savings we had left after purchasing the gym. *We needed to cut our household expenses further, or I had to give up on my dream.*

We decided to sell our home and purchase a small condo for under $100,000 in the same town as the gym. We cut our mortgage payment in half and permanently saved on travel and meals. We finally started sleeping in our actual beds, and our household budget was back to breakeven! This only happened because we understood our monthly expenses and were willing to scale back our lifestyle to keep the gym alive. Our monthly budget allowed for a weekly dinner date costing no more than $30.00. But...

Hitting rock bottom financially was waiting around the corner.

I was working 80 hours a week at the gym. At the start of the second year, our books were in the red for $20,000, and our savings account was empty. Even with all the up-front planning and use of the monthly budget, we ran out of money after purchasing the new plate-loaded equipment for the gym. That's the risk of being an entrepreneur. It's the universe's way of testing your commitment to following your Purpose.

I would have lost the gym without the $35,000 loan from my parents to cover the shortfall and provide some working capital to get us through another busy season. I was out of money, but I just needed a little more time. The gym membership was growing and would soon be profitable for us. That $35,000 loan allowed me to own the gym for another 17 years! It was the turning point for me.

When you decide to go Against the Grain and follow your own Path in life, you must understand the bare financial minimum to keep a roof over your head and food on the table. Start living beneath your means from the day you land your first job. Develop this discipline as a Path toward your own Freedom. It doesn't matter how much or little you make. You will hit rock bottom financially while going Against the Grain. Count on it. It was part of the process for nearly every person I know who is stubborn enough to follow their Purpose against all odds and succeed.

Michael and Marc Grondahl lived in the gym they purchased before figuring out the formula for Planet Fitness. Pete Roberts lived off borrowed money from family and friends before deciding to start Origin USA. Paul Mecurio lived out of his car while transitioning from Wall Street investment banker to stand-up comedian. Andy Frisella slept on dirty cots with his partner in the back of their supplement store and made only $65,000 during his first five years in business creating 1st Phorm. Mat Fraser purposely lived with his parents and used a basement gym to reduce his living expenses. He focused purely on winning the CrossFit Games. Cutting expenses is not a necessity for living your Purpose, but it is likely. Society's Box creates comforts so no one questions the lies. Going Against the Grain isn't comfortable, but it is worth it. To succeed, you simply have to prepare in advance.

Create your monthly budget and look for areas where you can "trim the fat" before you kick down the walls of Society's Box. Run the various financial scenarios that could happen during your journey. Don't blindly jump off the fence. To live an Authentic Life, you must be willing to reach rock bottom financially and *not give up*. Grow accustomed to living beneath your means, and you'll be emotionally strong enough to keep moving forward when the going gets tough. If you're still worried about keeping up with the Joneses, you'll hop right back onto Society's Path at the first sign of trouble.

With a clear Vision for your Purpose and how to achieve it without fear, and with a plan for Freedom, it's time to understand why some people who go Against the Grain seemingly do everything right and are well prepared for the climb, but never find Freedom.

It's a mistake you don't want to make.

CHAPTER 8

DO YOU REALLY NEED MORE?

"Get used to dining out without the crowds, to being a slave to fewer slaves, to getting clothes only for their real purpose, and to living in more modest quarters."

—SENECA

"How in the hell can someone with your business background and talents only own one Planet Fitness location?! You are one of the smartest franchisees we have in the system. You live in a small townhouse and drive your Planet Fitness lettered van. Don't you want the big new house, sports car, and way more income so your wife doesn't have to work any longer?" asked Michael. My response was simple: "Nope! I have a great life. It's simple and carefree. I love the Freedom I have to do the things I enjoy in life."

Michael Grondahl, one of the Planet Fitness founding brothers, was always trying to get me to open additional Planet Fitness locations. But three years before this phone call, I had divorced myself from the world of "more is better." My view of success no longer meshed with Society's desires. I had learned a vital lesson at a young age.

Enough is an important word, critical to finding Freedom. Freedom is created by keeping things small and simple. It's counterintuitive, but getting promoted too many times or growing your business too large can remove the fun you had in the beginning when things were small.

Once you get "VP" stamped on your business card, suddenly it's only acceptable to live in a particular neighborhood. It's only proper to drive certain automobiles and send your children to certain private schools. These are the lies Society wants you to believe. These are the lies that chain you to your job or business. Society keeps whispering in your ear, "Take the next promotion (to a position you don't even want), or expand your business (to a size that requires increased management). You'll finally have enough money to enjoy your life." I am here to tell you: *more* is just a lie.

Michael, a friend prior to franchising Planet Fitness, admits the driving force behind Planet Fitness was his desire to make more money than his father did during his best year in business. It was all about being successful in Society's eyes. Bigger homes, faster cars, and the status that comes with entrepreneurial success. After the partners sold Planet Fitness to a private equity group, Michael asked if I would be interested in moving my family to New Hampshire to partner with him in other business ventures.

My wife and I had just had our daughter, Brenna, and my parents had recently moved from Maine to help us with babysitting. I loved the life I had created and let Michael know it would be tough for me to move to New Hampshire. As much as I relished the prospect of trying something new with him, the timing wasn't right to uproot my entire family. His response was as follows:

From: Mike

To: Craig

Sent: Thursday, August 9, 2012

Craig trust me, I respect that more than anything. You truly understand what is important, and trust me, $$$$$ is overrated. Most people look at me and say how lucky I am. It is true, but it is because my family loves me. I have healthy kids and I am still somewhat healthy. Money makes people treat you differently, and after time it makes you paranoid. You always wonder if people like you for who you are, or for what you have...it has been tough on Eric (Mike's oldest son) because his friends have him taking them out to dinner every night and he doesn't know how to say no. You don't need to apologize for doing the right thing. If I had to do it over, I would have gone your approach rather than mine. My life has been miserable since 07 and yeah, I'm worth 200 million, but I don't see my kids, I'm in a bad mood, and the stress has my back so tight I lay on the couch all weekend and need pain pills to get thru my week.

I thought if I accomplished X, Y, & Z then I'd be happy...but I became angry when I accomplished everything I thought GOD wanted me to. Then I just became disillusioned with being rich. I was pissed because I wasn't happy, yet I had done all the work. I'm lost. I'm wealthy, but it's like I finished the race with no one else there, and it makes me feel very alone. You are a rich man because to me, you have the wisdom to choose what is important and not look back. I may have the accolades, but I am miserable. You have the answer. Don't feel bad for doing the right thing...I am proud of you! I hope someday you can make me understand what is wrong.

Your friend,

Mike

Maybe Mike hadn't been lucky enough to have a person in his life like my maternal grandfather. A person of modest means who had never lived in anything nicer than his single-wide trailer. Someone who had figured out that a successful life wasn't about money and material things. It was about being happy with what you could afford and surrounding yourself with people you loved, who loved you back. My grandfather enjoyed the simple things in life. His passions included a night of playing cards, the Friday night bowling league, and his favorite pastime of all: a round of golf. I can't elaborate enough about what a wonderful and simple man my maternal grandfather was. I don't know why he had such an impact on my life, but I think it may have been because he was the opposite of my father.

People stuck in Society's Box point to the bigger house they just bought and the latest sports car or luxury SUV they just leased as justification for staying in an unfulfilling career that demands most of their waking hours. The weekend round of golf at the country club and the upcoming vacation to Europe become the sustenance to get through their day-to-day existence as some corporate clone. After a series of promotions, it eventually becomes impossible to carve out any personal time to do the things they love in life. They become a cog in the system of climbing the corporate ladder. For every rung they climb, the job becomes less and less rewarding.

I know some "corporate world" specialists who have said no to promotions so they could keep doing what they love. I know some business owners who refrain from opening another location or producing another product line so they can keep their business at a manageable size. They want to maintain plenty of personal time for themselves and their families. I was one of them.

Can you guess which people live happier and more fulfilling lives? Our Society's problem is that it's rare to find people who understand when to say "enough." Society rewards the person with a more prominent title, higher income, and a bigger home. I learned early in life how the constant desire for more can lead to a very unfulfilling life.

All I had to do was watch my father.

My father and mother both grew up poor in northeastern Connecticut. Neither had more than a high school education. Mom grew up in a single-wide trailer and was very book smart, while Dad grew up on a farm and was gifted with a high level of common sense and street smarts.

Soon after my mother graduated from high school, she and my dad got married, and my mom had my brother at the ripe old age of 20. Two years later, I entered the universe. My mom spent the next fifteen years staying at home and caring for her children. She was a terrific mother, full of love and willing to do anything for us. She never associated with being poor as a child. Even though my grandmother died of a heart attack when my mother was only 27, my mom's view of the world came from a father who loved his simple life. Thankfully, she had learned the opposite of Society's lies.

My father grew up poor on a farm in Pomfret, Connecticut. I remember him telling my brother and me how he had to take his bath using the same hot water as his three other siblings. His two sisters always went first, followed by his younger brother. My father went last in the cold and dirty water. We heard the stories of how he hated going to school after milking the cows and feeding the livestock. He smelled of cow shit, and all the kids made fun of him. Due to his upbringing and poor relationship with his father, my dad had a single-minded focus his entire life. His mission was to prove to everyone he wasn't the poor kid that smelled like cow shit from the farm anymore.

Over time, I understood my dad was trying to prove that fact to *himself*.

My father worked the hardest to get the next available promotion from his first job in the local Putnam mills. Every promotion meant more money to spend on better cars and clothes. Higher social status was the overriding goal for my dad. He became a salesman at the local Ford & Mercury dealership in town. Charlie Perkins excelled as a salesman and loved getting a brand-new dealer car to drive each year.

With his outstanding work ethic and outgoing personality, he eventually became the Ford dealership's general manager. He worked long hours Monday through Friday, and a half-day every Saturday. My dad focused his early work life on saving enough money to purchase 63 acres in East Putnam and begin what would become a 15-year journey of creating his very own plantation, on the backs of his two sons. From Saturday at 1:00 p.m. through Sunday at nightfall, my father spent every spare minute of his time creating a homestead that appeared to be owned by someone with much more wealth than our family had. It was never-ending work for my brother and me.

It started with building a raised ranch situated on a small clearing, some 300 feet from the road. The house was initially hidden from the road by the thick woods surrounding it. My brother and I were too small to understand what our future held. We simply loved the fact we had all those woods to play in. Eventually, the woods surrounding our house were replaced by acres of lawn, giving a full view of what honestly looked like a plantation to anyone driving by. Behind our new raised ranch stood a sizeable hand-built barn that housed our snowmobiles, dirt bikes, John Deere tractor, and all of its lawn care and wood cutting attachments. We needed them to cut the golf course-sized lawn and haul 12 cord of wood out of our 63 acres of woodland each year.

A built-in swimming pool with a screened-in cabana was

to the house's right, surrounded by a hand-planted fence of hemlock trees. To the left of the house was a hand-built open-air canopy for stacking the 12 cord of split wood we hauled out of our land each year.

My father's life centered on impressing everyone around him. He was desperate to have people believe he was more successful and wealthy than he was. Instead of finding any sort of Freedom in his life, my father lived his life like a slave to Society's expectations. He worked 65 hours a week at the car dealership, and then from dusk till dawn on the weekends at our home. My brother and I only spent time with him on the weekends, as we tried in vain to get all the projects on his checklist crossed off by Sunday night.

You may wonder how my father's life concluded. After selling the "plantation" and its 63 acres along with a small TV and radio store my parents owned at the end of their working lives, my father and mother had accumulated over $900,000 in investment holdings. But even in retirement, my father couldn't rein in his spending. After years of buying and upgrading retirement homes in Connecticut and Florida and purchasing a new vehicle every other year, my parents' financial advisor, Len, had to make a last-ditch effort to provide them with enough money to survive.

I remember sitting in the meeting at Len's office where he implored my parents to purchase an annuity with their last $400,000 and downsize their base living expenses to the size of their combined Social Security checks. The income from the annuity would be their "spending" money. The crazy spending was over. My mother asked Len what would be left for my brother and me. Len apologetically replied, "Nothing."

My father lived the final years of his life in a tiny senior income-adjusted apartment. My parents went from owning what honestly looked like an estate on 63 acres to living in an apartment the size of their old living room. All because my father never learned the meaning of *enough*.

In many cases, having more takes you further away from personal Freedom. Freedom in life starts with having the financial ability to cover your essential monthly household expenses: a roof over your head, food on the table, and adequate medical insurance. It expands to saving 10 to 15 percent for retirement, and having enough life insurance to cover a catastrophe. Children may require a 529 plan for their college education. Add in some form of long-term care insurance so you don't become a burden to the ones you love, and you've got your financial house in order.

Bigger homes and fancier cars should never come before covering these basics. When they do, it's critical to realize you're going down the wrong Path! You may want more, but recognize that it stems from believing Society's lies. Spend your savings on experiences that will last a lifetime, not on bigger homes and more expensive cars to impress the neighbors. Pick up that hobby you've always wanted to try. Enjoy simple activities that cost little to nothing at all. They will have a more lasting impact on your life than the new five-bedroom home with his and her Range Rovers parked in the driveway. When your energy centers on keeping up with the Joneses, things can go wrong in a hurry.

Here's a cautionary tale from the business world.

Our first Islands of Success Management Consulting client was a small sheet metal manufacturing company, recently purchased by a "downsized" corporate executive. The new owner, let's call him Dick, was a typical vice president-level executive used to having many employees beneath him to do the required work. Dick was an excellent sales-man, great at sweet-talking a customer into doing business, but he had no idea what it took to make a factory perform.

Dick had the brains to know he needed help fixing the higher-volume factory's production and inventory control problems. Dick hired Islands of Success at an acceptable hourly rate. I headed to the factory floor while Elliot dove into the plant's performance reporting and inventory con-trol systems.

Over the next 12 months, we implemented pull production and lean manufacturing systems. Workers were organized into teams and given the training required to handle daily problems on their own. We installed new raw material ordering systems. Raw material and work-in-process inventory levels dropped by over $1 million on an annual basis. Defect levels dropped to under 1 percent, and on-time delivery reached 98 percent. The bottom line improved by over $500,000 annually. The new owner found himself with a small sheet metal fabricating company producing high profits on a repeatable basis. The future looked bright.

Unfortunately, Dick still had something to prove.

He was adamant about getting back the lifestyle he had lost after his ouster from Corporate America. Dick sold his upscale home, purchased a condo, and lived a lifestyle well beneath what he had been accustomed to when he was a vice president. Dick should have continued living a down-sized life to mesh better with the new realities of small business ownership. Instead, Dick used his business's greatly improved profitability to purchase a much larger sheet metal factory located over an hour away. His goal was to move the existing high-volume production lines into the larger factory and reap the benefits of improved economies of scale.

Dick was a firm believer in the business philosophy of "If

you aren't growing, you're dying." He had "friends" in the banking industry who allowed him to purchase the larger company almost entirely on debt. The expansion came just after I decided to move away from the consulting practice and buy World Gym. I'd had enough of dealing with the tremendous egos of guys like Dick. Dick was fine with my decision and hired my partner, Elliot, as the full-time CFO to oversee the merger of the new company and manage its bottom line.

The team moved the smaller factory into the larger plant, and initially things looked great. The same systems used to turn around the first plant's performance improved the combined factory's profitability. Dick celebrated by selling his condo and buying a mansion in West Hartford, Connecticut, and new vehicles for himself and his wife. Dick was finally able to send his son to an expensive private school. Dick's comeback was complete! He was back to keeping up with the Joneses and proving everyone wrong about his corporate ouster.

Dick must have forgotten about all that debt on the books.

When a couple of large customers permanently switched from metal to plastic components, demand fell, and Dick began struggling to make loan payments to the bank. He needed his large draw to pay for all the personal debt his family had recently acquired, and he was unwilling to sell the big house and get rid of the car leases to help lessen the financial drain on the company.

When the largest customer reduced the size of their ongoing orders, it became impossible for Dick to pay back the loan. He tried everything to find new customers, but many had moved to plastic components, and his calls fell on deaf ears. The bank called in the loan, and Dick lost the company. The mansion and cars got repossessed—a tragedy caused by the deadly combination of ego, greed, and the never-ending need for *more*.

In horror, I learned that Elliot had made a terrible decision to help Dick save the company and had personally signed a line of credit pledging his assets as collateral. The decision had been made without Elliot saying a word to me. Elliot also lost everything. This story illustrates the dangers of believing in Society's lies and living your life trying to keep up with the Joneses.

When the underlying goal for wealth and success is ego driven, the outcome has nothing to do with autonomy and peaceful living. The result is heavier and heavier chains locking you into a life where it's impossible to succeed, as there will always be someone else making more money than you.

When career promotions or business growth are the natural progressions of living authentically and following your Purpose, you won't be able to distinguish between work and play. You will have reached the summit on the Path called Against the Grain and cleared the Path for others behind you. Find your Freedom by helping others find theirs.

Success in life has little to do with creating individual wealth and status for ourselves. It has everything to do with assisting others in succeeding by doing the things that give you goose bumps. As Jesse Itzler so perfectly states on the *3-of-7 Podcast* with Chadd Wright, "Follow the Path that touches your SOUL!" Jesse goes on to speak about finishing The Hennepin Hundred run in 2019:

"A lot of people have asked me why I still do challenging races. They say, 'Why aren't you on a beach?' Here you go...I've sold three companies in my lifetime: one to Coca-Cola, one to Warren Buffet's NetJets, and one to a public company (SFX), all before I was basically forty. When the wires hit the account, it felt amazing...but I'm telling you from my heart, those money transfers didn't touch the soul like this race did. The reality is, nothing touches the soul like experiences. You don't get the emotion and brotherhood we felt here any other way."

Remember this on your quest for Freedom. If getting "ahead" is all about *you* and personal success, you'll never break free from the chains Society has clamped around your ankles. If you are always looking for *more*, it will be nearly impossible to free up your time to focus on the things that matter to you.

Don't give in to the constant temptation for more. It's usually a trap. It creates a vicious cycle of believing happiness is the feeling you get when you buy that new pair of shoes. You work harder, put in more hours, and the joy comes flooding in when the dealer hands you the keys to your brand-new sports car. You accept the next promotion and no longer have time to hit the gym most nights after work, but you can finally save the down payment for your first home. You're following Society's Path, and it sure feels like success. Everyone is patting you on the back.

Eventually, you accept a promotion and find yourself at a management level where you see firsthand who's running the corporation. You're not impressed or even motivated by the upper management team, but you keep your mouth closed and feel good about the salary increase you just received. You're married now with a newborn, living in a home you never believed you would own. But something weird has entered your psyche. You start to dread going to work on Monday. Nothing at work gives you goose bumps anymore. So, you begin buying more toys. More distractions.

Even though you're up to your eyeballs in debt, the Harley-Davidson helps you forget about work. The vacation home provides a temporary place to go to "get away from it all." But the momentary high can never overcome living a life that doesn't resonate with your soul.

I've done my best to shine a light on the fact of how easy it is to get shackled within Society's Box. *Status. Wealth. Power.* On your deathbed, they all mean nothing. During your lifetime, they typically don't even last. No one is going to remember what size home you lived in or the type of car you drove. What's the obsession with keeping up with the Joneses? You're trading your Freedom and working for the man while mindlessly buying things to make yourself look better to others. You're fooling yourself into thinking you're happy. It's important to admit you've been living a lie.

Ryan Holiday perfectly captures the essence of this message in his excellent book *Stillness Is the Key.* He tells the story of Kurt Vonnegut and Joseph Heller attending a fancy party in New York. As the two of them stand in the home of some billionaire, Vonnegut needled his friend. "Joe," he said, "how does it feel to know that our host may have made more money yesterday than your novel has earned in its entire history?"

"I've got something he can never have," Heller replied.

"And what on earth could that be?" Vonnegut asked.

"The knowledge that I've got enough."

But the battle to live your Authentic Life isn't over just yet.

—

CHAPTER 9

THE LAST MILE IS ALWAYS THE LEAST CROWDED

"If you're going through hell, keep going."

—WINSTON CHURCHILL

"Can't you just sell this stupid gym and get another plant manager job?" Gina said while wiping tears from her face as we ate our Sunday dinner after working at the gym all day. It had been two years since I'd purchased World Gym. The constant lack of discretionary income, combined with working 60-plus hours a week at the gym, had worn her willpower down to the bone. She had recently met with a therapist who prescribed a mild anti-depressant to help her cope with the stress of being a small business owner.

I had given up a six-figure income as a plant manager and was paying myself $1,000 per month to help cover the mortgage and taxes on the small condo we had purchased near the gym. Gina had recently left her job as an early morning cook at a convalescent home to become gym manager so we could keep the most significant portion of payroll within our household. Together we were grossing just under $50,000 per year, and the change to our lifestyle was hitting my wife hard.

I remember feeling empty walking into the gym later that night after my wife begged me to sell it and get another job as a plant manager. I always went into the gym on Sunday nights when we were closed so I could work with no interruptions. I turned on the lights, and instead of turning on the office computer, I sat down on one of the wooden bar stools at our juice bar. Was all this work and stress worth it?

I thought back to the crazy amount of work and effort it had taken to turn around multiple departments in that old Standard Plant. This was the same amount of work and stress, but everything was on the line. This time I owned the asset that was producing so much stress in my life. I still remember sitting on one of the wooden stools at the juice bar, looking up toward heaven, and asking my Grandpa Louie for advice.

"What should I do, Gramps?" I asked with tears running down my cheeks. I knew that sticking to my Path of owning this gym wasn't healthy for my marriage. But I also understood on a deeper level that giving up and jumping back in line with Society's herd would be even worse. On that lonely night at the gym, I decided to do everything I could to save it and eventually create the life of autonomy I needed. I mentally blew up the bridge that led back to Society's Path.

Without the level of commitment forged that lonely night at the gym, I would never have lived a life filled with Freedom. There were so many reasons to give up during the early years of owning the gym. A wife on antidepressants hating the drastic drop in disposable income within our household. A wife who would eventually look me in the face and say, "I don't even like you anymore," in place of the usual kiss before bed and saying, "I love you." Bouncing a rent check and learning the checkbook was $20,000 in the red. A brand-new Gold's Gym opening a mile down the road and losing 25 percent of my membership base.

Going Against the Grain will always test your resolve. The myriad of obstacles will tempt you to throw in the towel when the times get tough. It's so important to understand your *why* before jumping on this Path. It's why it's critical to take the time to determine your Purpose before breaking out of Society's Box.

My first marriage ended during the tumultuous early years of owning the gym. I borrowed $35,000 from my parents just in time to keep the power from being shut off, and it ended up keeping the doors open for another 17 years. I converted from World Gym to Planet Fitness when Gold's Gym opened a new location a mile down the street and watched my membership grow from 1,000 to over 5,000 members. Each decision to move forward was more challenging than I could ever explain. But I loved my gym and helping others regain their health through fitness, so I just kept looking for ways to succeed. If I was going to fail, I was going down swinging.

If you've made it this far through the book, I believe you are committed to pursuing your Purpose and finding your Freedom. Before starting down this challenging Path called Against the Grain, you must embrace the **Fifth Guiding Principle** for living an autonomous life. When your logical brain says, "Move on, this just isn't working!" but your heart says, "We're almost there, don't give up!" listen to your heart. Every. Single. Time. Life will always give you one last big hurdle to overcome before you get to taste the fruit of your labors. I believe it's a universal truth for anyone who takes the Path called Against the Grain. Perseverance in the face of obstacles is a prerequisite to living an Authentic Life.

I can tell you from firsthand experience when you reach the "should I stay or should I go" point in your journey, it's hard to see how close you are to succeeding. Success is usually right around the next corner, yet many people throw in the towel because they can't see around the bend. Going Against the Grain requires you to embrace what gives you goose bumps, move through your fears, live beneath your means, develop the discipline to put work before pleasure, and persevere in the face of every obstacle until you reach your destination.

There is no such thing as "instant success." No one sees the struggle and tears that come before the success because most successful people don't like to talk about how close they came to quitting along the way. I came close to giving up and going back to Corporate America more times than I can count. The toughest test came when my friends, the founders of Planet Fitness, sold their company to private equity—I knew change was coming.

With a private equity goal of taking the company public, revenue streams needed to grow. Being a single-unit owner within such a large franchise structure made my location a liability, not an asset. Planet Fitness Corporate started exercising its right to make particular locations expand and even relocate to acquire a successor franchise. I worried my site could end up finding its way onto that list.

After the sale of Planet Fitness to private equity, Michael Grondahl asked if I would be interested in accepting a sweat-equity position to partner in the startup of a brand-new indoor trampoline park in Portsmouth, New Hampshire. Michael had recently purchased a building and started construction of the trampoline park. He had partnered with Mark, a family friend, to run the park's day-to-day operations once it opened. Michael knew Mark had never owned or operated a business before, so he asked if I would be willing to guide and mentor Mark for a 25 percent equity stake in the park.

With the possibility of Planet Fitness Corporate requiring me to relocate and expand my gym, I was open to pursuing another course of action as a potential backup plan. I took Steph and Brenna to a couple of the new indoor trampoline parks that had just opened up in Rhode Island and Connecticut. While my three-year-old daughter loved every minute of each visit (what kid doesn't love to jump on trampolines and play arcade games?), I never spotted a single goose bump on either of my arms.

My gym was running well, and I had an outstanding staff I could count on, so I decided to take the risk. I agreed to become partners with Michael and Mark and to help open Blitz Indoor Trampoline Park. I started renting an old beach house from Michael's brother Marc in the spring of 2014 and began spending Sunday night through Thursday afternoon in Portsmouth, New Hampshire. When we were getting close to opening the doors of Blitz, my wife and daughter decided to move into the beach house with me permanently. Neither of them liked me being away all the time.

Stephanie sold her massage therapy business back in Connecticut, and Brenna started pre-kindergarten in Portsmouth, New Hampshire, in August of 2014. Blitz opened its doors in October as the first indoor trampoline park in New Hampshire. Business soared. Steph worked at Blitz around Brenna's school schedule to help offset lost household income from her massage therapy business. I still owned the townhouse and gym back in Connecticut, so I began traveling back every other Wednesday to meet with my staff and check on the condo. My parents still lived less than a mile away from my home in Connecticut, so they were always nearby to grab the mail and check on the house.

It wasn't easy running Blitz and managing the gym from afar, but Steph and I loved the change of scenery. We were living on the beach with our young daughter, Brenna, and golden retriever, Iris, and we were only a couple of hours from the splendor of the White Mountains. Portsmouth was a bustling little city filled with outstanding restaurants and fantastic stores. We had fallen in love with New Hampshire.

In the spring of 2015, we decided to sell our townhouse in

Connecticut. Blitz was doing much better than expected, the gym hadn't missed a beat without me being around daily, and Steph and I loved the idea of starting a new chapter in our lives. The goal was to franchise this new indoor trampoline park and eventually sell my gym in Connecticut, following a new Path forward in New Hampshire. We put our Connecticut townhouse on the market and started looking for a house in New Hampshire.

Everything aligned perfectly. Our townhouse sold the same week we put a down payment on a new house in New Hampshire. The moving company picked up our belongings in Connecticut and delivered them to our new home in New Hampshire the next day. We moved into our new home in early August of 2015, and Brenna began kindergarten at one of the best K–8 school systems in the state.

It seemed too good to be true.

My family and I decided to move to New Hampshire based on Blitz's initial success, combined with my ability to oversee my gym back in Connecticut. As partners, Michael, Mark, and I were hoping to create a recurring revenue membership model like we had at Planet Fitness, but no matter how hard we tried, a low-cost monthly membership never gained traction at Blitz.

A monthly membership meant kids wanted to go to Blitz

all the time, and there was nothing for the parent to do but sit on some uncomfortable bleacher seats for hours on end. After just a year of operation, revenues fell by over 40 percent as the business's initial appeal started to fade. Profitability settled to a point where Blitz supplied a decent salary for a single owner. The indoor trampoline park franchise idea wasn't gaining any traction.

During this realization, Planet Fitness Corporate notified me I had to relocate my gym to a better retail location and expand its size to fit my area's demographics in order to sign another 10-year franchise agreement. You already know what we decided to do next. I sold my shares of Blitz to my other partners, and that sale was complete in October of 2016. Steph and I signed our Sola franchise agreement in March of 2017. The search to find the best possible location in New Hampshire for our first Sola began in April of 2017.

Do you remember how important it is to start the process of finding Freedom covered in goose bumps?

Now I was faced with an even more significant dilemma. Was I going to sell my gym after 18 years of ownership or try to move it? The gym provided a large portion of our household income, and I had just sold the income stream coming in from Blitz. How long was it going to take to find a commercial space for our first Sola? How long would it take to complete the buildout and get the first-ever salon suite concept to full occupancy in the state of New Hampshire? I loved my gym and my employees. How would I ever part with such a significant portion of my life? When I needed it most, the voice in my heart spoke to me again and said, "Craig, remember the process that has always led you to Freedom":

- Listen to your Authentic Self.
- Embrace the work.
- Move toward your fear.
- Live beneath your means.
- Know when to say "enough."
- Don't give up.

I had found the only location in Enfield, Connecticut, empty and large enough to hold a new 20,000-square-foot Planet Fitness. Corporate approved the relocation. It was in the Enfield Mall, located right in the center of town. But the Enfield Mall was in steady decline. Store after store was either closing or moving out. Steph and I needed to make a hard decision: move the gym or sell it. We came up with a simple plan to help us make a final decision.

Steph and I agreed to drive back to Connecticut and walk the mall's entirety without speaking a word to each other. At the end of the tour, we would decide yes or no to spending $2 million to move the gym to the Enfield Mall.

We drove back to Connecticut together. As we walked out of the mall that day, we looked at each other and simultaneously said, "No." There were so many closed stores; the mall looked like a ghost town. With tears in my eyes, I put the gym up for sale the very next day. It was May of 2017, and it was one of the most difficult decisions I had ever made. I loved the fitness business and the staff at my gym. But it didn't make sense to risk $2 million to move the gym to a questionable location. It made much more sense to sell my gym and use the capital to support Steph and her new love called Sola.

The pressure was on. Steph and I had no idea what a painstakingly slow process searching for our first Sola location would be. The gym sold in December of 2017, and we were nowhere close to finding a commercial site that worked for a Sola. Sola Corp had warned us that finding an acceptable lease was the most challenging part of the Sola process, but we never thought in a million years that after seven months of constant searching, we would still be standing empty-handed. Now we had also lost the monthly income from the gym!

I picked up some consulting work in early 2018 to keep us from tapping into the proceeds from the sale of the gym. It became harder and harder not to succumb to becoming an employee again. We couldn't find an acceptable commercial lease in New Hampshire. Winter turned to spring, and we deemed another couple of potential locations as unacceptable. Spring turned to summer, and we were ready to jump off the Piscataqua River Bridge. It had now been well over a year since we signed our franchise agreement, and Steph and I just looked at each other in bewilderment.

I remember asking our commercial realtor about a local CrossFit gym situated in a great retail location. I had noticed the parking lot was always empty. Our realtor learned the CrossFit lease was nearing completion, and the owners weren't renewing. Corporate labeled it an excellent location for a Sola. It was September of 2018, *eighteen months* after signing our franchise agreement.

After three months of negotiating with the landlord, we signed a 10-year lease with two five-year options in December of 2018, one year after we sold the gym. We finally found the best location for a Sola in New Hampshire. It was only a 10-minute drive from our home, and where Steph was currently working as a massage therapist. Steph would be able to open her massage studio right within the walls of our Sola! We had persevered for 21 months and finally found a location.

Little did we know, the obstacles had just begun.

The CrossFit lease expired on May 31, 2019, and the CrossFit owner had told us back in September of 2018 that he already had another location for his gym. He told us the landlord approved letting them out of their lease early, once we had signed our deal. We should have known better. CrossFit was merely using Sola as a wedge to get out of their lease early *if they wanted to*. We learned later that CrossFit hadn't even started lease negotiations with their new location. Plus, they still needed time to complete their buildout.

Stephanie and I didn't take possession of the site until June 1, 2019. *Twenty-six months after signing our franchise agreement.* Spots suddenly appeared on my face where hair would no longer grow. But, we could finally begin the 120-day construction period quoted by Sola Corp's recommended builder.

The obstacles were gaining momentum.

Early into the construction process, we got a phone call from our general contractor. "Something is wrong here," he stated. "You both need to stop over and see this for yourselves." The crew had demolished the CrossFit buildout and was in the process of cutting out sections of the cement floor to accurately lay in the gravity-fed piping that would connect each sink within the 20 salon studios to the main sewer line in the back of the building.

When Steph and I entered the site to meet with our general contractor, he walked us to the rear of the building, where the main sewer line was supposed to be. The plumbers had dug down five feet in every direction, and the only thing they found was a connecting pipe that went to the main sewer line. The main sewer line was located 150 feet away on the other side of the building.

The connecting pipe was only eight inches deep! We needed at least 36 inches to ensure the gravity flow of wastewater from the sinks within all the 20 studios. It was back to the drawing board. Our construction company had to reengineer the entire plumbing system to include a large pit filled with two ejector pumps. The wastewater would have to be pumped to the main sewer line. The change cost us over a month in delays and loads of extra money.

We opened the doors to Sola Portsmouth on December 5, 2019. *Thirty-two months after signing the franchise agreement. Twenty-four months after selling my gym.*

It would have been so easy to quit along the way.

We opened Sola Portsmouth with eight of the 20 salon studios preleased. Stephanie took Studio 12 and opened her own business, Unravel Therapeutic Massage. At the end of 2019, we had nine of the 20 salon studios leased. Then 2020 rolled in. Interest came back after the holidays, and Stephanie leased another four studios. We had 13 out of 20 studios rented by the end of February.

Someone must have thought it was time to test our perseverance thoroughly.

It was March 2020, and COVID-19 was suddenly upon us. Schools were closing down. Sola Portsmouth was closed by government mandate in late March. We stopped collecting rent from our Sola Pros when we couldn't allow them access to their businesses. Our landlord only agreed to defer our rent until December. We didn't have any employees, so we didn't qualify for any PPE loans.

Maybe it *was* finally time to quit?

The Sola Portsmouth leasing phone started ringing—and it didn't stop. When we were allowed to reopen in late May, we did so with 20 out of 20 studios leased! The panic around the pandemic pushed beauty professionals toward the safety of an individual salon studio. Sola offered a one-on-one salon experience, easily cleaned and sanitized between each client. Who would have ever guessed?

When it seemed like we would never find a location to open our first Sola, I remember calling myself a dumbass for selling my interest in Blitz. I beat myself up even more for selling my gym in Connecticut. I hit one of the lowest points in my life during the two years of searching for our first Sola location. I had given up everything to start over in a state where my family wanted to live, and nothing was going my way. Throughout this painful process, I focused on helping my wife realize her dream. I focused on creating a new life for my wife and young daughter. A life that would eventually be full of autonomy with the ability to enjoy whatever passion bubbled to the top of their fun meter. Thank God I didn't quit.

> Blitz Indoor Trampoline Park closed its doors for good in August 2020, after reopening for only a month. Planet Fitness of Enfield, Connecticut, closed for over three months due to COVID-19 and lost 20 percent of its members. All the doubt and self-sabotage over the previous two years proved unfounded once again.

My life has gone through a 180-degree evolution. I find myself in a supporting role each day. I am the one getting our daughter up and off to school. I'm the one making sure I am back home from my consulting work when Brenna gets off the bus so I can help her with her homework. I am an assistant coach for my daughter's soccer, basketball, and lacrosse teams. After all these years, I am back to my original love. Coaching.

There's a lesson to learn from this chapter: *it's always easier to start something than it is to finish it.* There is no such thing as instant success in life. Many people start down the Path to living an Authentic Life, but few have the discipline and persistence to finish what they started. The critical requirements for staying on the Path called Against the Grain are high self-confidence and a willingness to endure when things get complicated. Obstacles are put in your Path to test your commitment. Learn to see them for what they are: a test of your will to keep moving forward. Success rewards the person who doesn't give up.

There have been many excellent books written with lessons to help you create the mental toughness to persevere in the face of daunting odds. In his outstanding book *Can't Hurt Me*, David Goggins describes the "cookie jar" he created to boost his confidence to move forward when all seemed lost. David fills his cookie jar with all the times he has overcome obstacles and succeeded in reaching his goals. It's excellent advice. Whenever I feel my confidence waning, I read the article "Don't Say Perkins Too Small" as a source to renew my will to persevere. I look at the plaque I received from the 500 employees from UAW Local 1645 when I left my job as plant manager. I think of the continued friendships I have with each manager I've had throughout the 18 years of owning my gym.

You need to fill your cookie jar if you hope to stay on the Path of going Against the Grain. The process of finding your Freedom is a long and demanding expedition. People are going to talk behind your back and make you feel insecure. You will get knocked down along the way. No one is going to pick you up. Use your cookie jar to remember who you are and what you are capable of doing.

Putnam Back Runs Big

Don't Say Perkins Too Small

High Schools
By
Dave Davis

Craig Perkins just might be Putnam High's answer to that biblical giant-killer, "David". Or at least that's the way it looks when the diminutive back takes the field against opposing "Goliaths".

Perkins, Putnam's flashy-running back who is currently the area's leading scorer in the high school football ranks, is 5-7 and weighs in at 158 pounds. It seems he is virtually risking his life every time he carries the ball.

However, just like "David" in the Bible, Perkins has mastered the knack of slaying his opponents — that is with some help from his bigger friends.

The Clipper co-captain has rushed for 973 yards through the first seven games of the season, and is a good bet to surpass the 1,000 yard barrier this Saturday against Windham Tech — needing only 27 yards.

Last year, as a junior, Perkins looked like he was headed for the 1,000 yard total, but with three games remaining and 780 yards already piled up, he came down with mono and was finished for the season.

Perkins worked out over the summer on a Universal weight lifting machine to improve his strength, and also took on an added responsibility this year, leading the team along with quarterback Chris Scraba (the other co-captain).

Perkins looks on leadership as another challenge, not much unlike running with the pigskin.

"You gotta keep the team together," said the personable Perkins, who went on to explain that most of the players have been together since their freshman year and are pretty close-knit.

The long run is Perkins' favorite, and understandably so. His quickness and acceleration permits him to run outside and beat most defenders, while he is also quite adept at running up the middle and rolling off tackles to break loose.

Clipper Coach Bob Deveau may have discovered the best way to describe Perkins' running ability.

"He never gets a solid hit," stated the Putnam mentor, "and that's probably the secret to his safety.

"He's real quick and durable and he takes a get's a lot of punishment," added Deveau. "His quickness is his biggest asset and he's shifty."

Not to be forgotten, though, are his blockers. Led by running back Danny Davis and left tackle Bart Ramon, his teammates take good care of him. Understandably, Perkins is the first one to realize this and anxiously gives credit where credit is due.

"It's got to be the blocking," said Perkins of his scoring success. "I've never had an injury."

Deveau also had laurels for the blockers. "Davis is a super blocker and Craig loves to follow him," said Deveau, also mentioning that Davis and Ramos help Perkins out tremendously down near the goal line.

The senior standout has rushed for 13 touchdowns, returned a kickoff 80 yards for a score, caught a 14-yard pass from Scraba for a 19th TD, and run for a pair of two-pointers totalling 94 points for the year.

His greatest effort of the season came in week No. 6 in the mud against Somers in a crucial Pequot Football Conference game when he rushed for 226 yards and scored three touchdowns, including a 34-yarder.

Perkins has been amazing his followers who considered him too small since he first started running the ball as a frosh, by constantly breaking tackles and carrying linebackers for five extra yards, and should continue to stun onlookers for the rest of the season also.

High School Happenings

In the scoring department for high school football Stonington holds the distinction of being the team with the most players having scored thus far with 11. Leading the scoring attack for the Bears is running back Phil Henkin with 24 points... On the other hand Plainfield is the team with the lowest amount of players to reach the end zone. Workhorse running back Randy Matteau leads the team with 76 points.

There have already been eight safeties recorded by local teams with Waterford and New London coming up with two of them, and East Lyme, Putnam, Windham Tech and Flich have each registered one... Individually

New London's John Green and Shaun Guess have both been credited with safeties.

Three area players have returned punts for touchdowns this year, and three have brought kickoffs all the way back for six points. East Lyme's Jim Drzewiecki has returned punts for TD's from 64 and 90 yards out, and Gary DuBose of Montville ran 74 yards with a punt return, while Joe Nowakowski of St. Bernard did the same for 65 yards. In the kickoff department, Craig Perkins of Putnam (80 yards), Doug DuBose of Montville (77 yards) and Stonington's Dave Donahue (60 yards), have all scored.

Four area defenders have brought interceptions all the way back for touchdowns, including Stonington's Dave Mitchell (100 yards), Chris Barber of Norwich (78 yards), St. Bernard's Tim Austin (35 yards) and Danny Davis of Putnam (18 yards)... three others have recovered fumbles in the end zone. They are Flich's Bob Keeler, and Joe Koehler and Bob McCarthy of Ledyard... four punts have been blocked and returned for scores. Green of New London has blocked two of these and run one in himself, while his teammate Guess ran the other in. Killingly's Mike Ricci and Steve Faucher of Putnam each own 35-yard returns of blocked punts.

Eight kickers have connected on field goal attempts this campaign, the longest of which belongs to Mike Pedojil of Griswold, a 40-yarder. East Lyme's Vinny LaGrotteria (25,23), Troy Cheatham of Flich (32,24), St. Bernard's Hank McCarthy (35,25) and Scott Crawford of Waterford (37,34) have two field goals apiece, and Lance Horne of Stonington (34), Windham's Jim Romano (33) and Howard Woodworth of Windham Tech (30) have one.

Perkins: Goliaths Beware

Living an Authentic Life is never easy. It's one of the most challenging endeavors anyone can try. Progress always comes slowly at the start. Going Against the Grain can be frustrating and unrewarding for long periods. It's normal to want to give up at the first signs of trouble and slip back into the comfort of Society's Box. Please don't. It's a trap.

Ninety-nine percent of the time, success in life goes to those who refuse to give up, regardless of the obstacles that block their Path. Commit now to becoming one of those people. Fill your cookie jar a little higher before attempting this arduous Path. But once you start down this Path, *don't give up*. Become an example of living an Authentic Life for all those you love. Be the light that illuminates the Path to living a life filled with autonomy!

The next chapter reveals the final step required to break out of Society's Box and live an Authentic Life filled with Freedom!

CHAPTER 10

IF YOU WANT TO OWN YOUR OWN LIFE, OWN YOUR OWN BUSINESS

"Measure your success by the growth of your Freedom."

—KYLIE FRANCIS

I felt my cell phone vibrate. I looked down at the screen: "Dad cell." It was late April of 2009, and Steph and I were entertaining her parents at our townhouse in Connecticut. My mom and dad were snowbirds and owned homes in both Maine and Florida. This time of year, they were preparing to head back to Maine for the summer months. They had moved from Connecticut to Maine to help when my brother's daughter Ashleen was born. I knew something was wrong before I even answered the call, because my dad never called.

"Hi, son. I've got some bad news. Your mom was hanging a lawn chair in the garage yesterday, and she fell from the top step on the ladder directly on her head, onto the cement floor. She fractured her skull and is at the hospital in serious condition." The emotion rose higher in his voice. "They aren't sure she's going to survive," my father stammered through his tears. "I talked to Chip earlier, and he is flying down tomorrow. Why don't you wait and see what happens over the next day or so while Chip is here?" I agreed and hung up the phone. I sat on our stairs with tears streaming down my face.

You may be wondering why I would start the last chapter of this book with this story. My decision to go Against the Grain and leave the corporate world had eventually resulted in me becoming the proud owner of a gym. My mom's accident occurred when I had owned my gym for nine years. By this stage of ownership, I had implemented excellent operating systems and had well-trained employees that enjoyed coming to work.

I had created the work environment I had always dreamed of. My employees knew I trusted them to run the gym as if it were their own; thus, the gym ran well without my constant involvement. Owning a business had given me the Freedom to continually explore all the different passions that found their way into my life, including an obsession with racing motocross, go-karts, and Brazilian

Jiu-Jitsu. I had created a life that allowed me to spend the next three months at Tampa General Rehab, playing an integral part in my mother's recovery from her traumatic brain injury.

The Path to gaining this autonomy wasn't an easy one. But, I learned a lot along the way. So, I wrote this book to help you find your way to Freedom. To live your life authentically and cage-free. This book is about creating a life filled with work that supports your *why*, provides enough money to enjoy the things in life you love to do, and gives you the time to do them. Autonomy rarely, if ever, happens with a typical nine-to-five.

If I had been okay with living under someone else's rules and following decisions I disagreed with, I could have survived in Corporate America. I was on the fast track to becoming an operations manager and potentially a Fortune 500 company vice president. To the outside world, I was on the "fast track." But Corporate America had too many antiquated rules to follow to climb their ladder of success. I craved *Freedom*.

Those first nine years working for the Torrington Company created some of the best experiences of my life. But it all changed in an instant, and I finally saw the shackles clamped around my ankles. I had a critical long-term decision to make: play by the rules and become what's typically called a "company man," or follow a new Path to live an Authentic Life. I learned a critical lesson along the way.

The ultimate act of Freedom is quitting! For most of the population, having a job, even the ones Society places on a pedestal like being a doctor, lawyer, engineer, or accountant, will never allow the picture on the cover of this book to become a reality. Freedom comes when you find yourself driving in the opposite direction of the nine-to-five traffic. Freedom comes when you have autonomy over what you do and think each day.

Ask yourself. Are you free?

To decide what you want to do on most days...

To do what you think is right in most situations...

To immerse yourself in projects or hobbies that you find interesting...

To spend time with people you want to spend time with...

To coach your kid's sports teams if you would like to...

To pursue *your* definition of success...

Without Freedom, what good is societal success? To have

Freedom in life, you need the ability to pay the bills and invest for the future, pursue work that gives Purpose to your life, and have the time to dedicate to your family *and* your passions. That's a whole life. That's an interesting life.

> The shortest Path to creating this life is owning your own business. I learned this lesson the hard way. I wrote this book to help save you from much of my pain and suffering.

I arranged this book's chapters in a checklist as a map for you to follow. Your journey starts with doing the work required to get your Vision clear as to what your business should be—to understand how important it is to select a business that resonates with your soul. Owning a UPS store because they make a lot of money doesn't make any sense if you don't enjoy packaging goods and working with the public. You've got to find the things that give you goose bumps. That's the starting point for the Path called Against the Grain. This process starts with an obsession for autonomy and ends with owning your own business. It's the shortest Path to Freedom I know.

Business ownership can take many forms. Businesses can range from consulting (low cost, low risk, and lower level of autonomy) to a boot-strapping startup where the founder has $10,000 and a great idea the market is just waiting for (low cost, high risk, high level of eventual autonomy). Going into business can mean purchasing an existing business and improving its performance (high price due to the value of its underlying assets and available cash flow, but less risk due to the same factors), or purchasing the rights to an established franchise (high cost due to the up-front and ongoing franchise fees, but the least risk due to a proven business model). I know the risks and benefits of all of these. Been there, done that, so to speak.

The key to finding my autonomy was owning a business with excellent operating systems and employees who were genuinely committed to my Vision. Remember this fact if your goal is to create Freedom in your life: the company must be able to operate daily without your direct involvement. If your goal is to have the free time to pursue activities you are passionate about, the business needs to make money when you are not there. If your business requires you to do all the work, you don't own a business; you own a job. It may be better than having a boss, but these businesses will limit the Freedom you enjoy.

When I finally decided to leave my job as plant manager, I started a consulting company with my friend Elliot. We called our new firm Islands of Success - Management Consulting and printed nice brochures and business cards. It was an easy way to enter the world of the self-employed. However, I eventually realized that consulting didn't give me the ability to call my own shots. The actual owner of each business still controlled the decision-making.

My obsession was to own my own manufacturing company and run it using the principles of success that had worked so well for me over the past nine years at the Standard Plant. But any manufacturing business that was for sale cost way more than Elliot and I could afford.

I needed to be the boss, running my own company. I wanted my own team.

Two years of consulting gave me the time to look closely at my life—too much time to be truthful. James Altucher has said that being authentic means finding a pain inside of you, teasing it out, and somehow solving it. So, what was the pain in my life driving me toward living a more Authentic Life?

The general pain in my life emanated from wanting to be my own boss and calling my own shots. That pain had reared its ugly head back at the Torrington Company when I lost all respect for my boss. But there was also acute pain driving change in my life. My acute pain came after my latest blood test revealed out-of-control blood lipid levels. My doctor clarified that if I didn't drastically change my lifestyle, I would likely have a heart attack before I was 50. Living an Authentic Life meant finding a way to solve my pain. In conjunction with building our new consulting practice and finding a business to own, I became obsessed with going to the gym and optimizing my diet. At 35, I fell back in love with fitness.

From working out with the plastic, sand-filled Joe Weider barbell set my dad had bought me as a kid, through endless days in the weight room while playing competitive sports, to a love of bodybuilding during my early corporate days, I had always loved fitness. Amid my frustration with consulting and the scare I received from my blood test, I became obsessed with fitness again. I studied for months and sat for the National Strength and Conditioning Association's Certified Personal Trainer (NSCA-CPT) Certification. I got in the best shape of my life. The proverbial light bulb switched on. Perhaps I could use the knowledge gained from improving my fitness to help others do the same?

A thought invaded my mind. What about owning a gym?! Goose bumps covered my body!

I searched online and read everything I could about purchasing and operating a gym. Finally, I came across a leading consultant specializing in the health club industry, Thomas Plummer. I bought his book *Making Money in the Fitness Industry* and read it from cover to cover. I needed to own a gym! I booked one of Thom's two-day "Business of Fitness" seminars in Myrtle Beach, South Carolina, and as life so often does when you finally commit to a Path, a door suddenly opened for me. During the seminar, I learned from Thom that he had a client looking to sell his World Gym located only an hour away from where I lived in Connecticut! Thom was brokering the deal and told me to get in a couple of workouts without telling anyone who I was and to let him know what I thought.

I remember the first time I walked through the doors of World Gym—Enfield. The gym was only three years old, and everything still looked new. All I could think of was owning this gym! I got in a good workout and took inventory of the equipment.

It was all I could talk about over dinner with my first wife, Gina. I told Elliot about the gym the next day and said I wanted to buy it. The gym owner offered to finance the sale, but he needed a large down payment to repay his existing equipment loans. I would have to cash in my 401(k) and lose 30 percent of its worth. But I still didn't have enough for the down payment. Elliot wasn't interested in owning a gym, but he offered to let me borrow what I needed to make the deal happen. After back-and-forth negotiations that lasted for months and had me ready to go back to being an employee, the gym was finally mine in December of 1999 for $318,600.

That may not seem like a lot of money to most, but for a 36-year-old guy from a blue-collar mill town, it was twice the value of the house I owned. I was finally the proud new owner of my own business for $118,600 down and a $200,000 five-year loan financed by the property owner!

I found a way to solve the pain inside me. I opened the door to my Authentic Life. I struggled greatly during my first three years of ownership. I ran out of money, lost 20 percent of my members to a new competitor, and ended up divorced. There were many times I thought the gym wasn't going to survive.

But I was doing something I loved, so I kept my head down and focused on doing the work—day after day after day. Eventually, I thrived. I developed detailed operating systems and trained my employees religiously. I gave them a direct voice in running the gym. Together we provided an outstanding customer experience. I owned that gym until December of 2017; 18 years. I created the personal time to pursue activities I was passionate about outside of work by training excellent managers who ran the gym like it was their own.

My life suddenly felt whole. I loved working at the gym. I loved teaching others how to exercise and eat correctly. But we all have interests and hobbies that fall outside the realm of work. When you combine what you love for work with doing what you love for play—all in the same day—you are living your Authentic Life.

My goal for writing this book is to help you do the same!

I found my Authentic Life unexpectedly. I wasn't even

looking for it. After purchasing the gym, I continued to live a singularly-focused life. My entire life revolved around the success of the gym. It was a very unbalanced life. After three years of struggling to improve the gym's performance, I finally took the time to visit my brother at his home in Maine. Chip was a veterinarian and owned a small practice in a rural town in Maine. He had recently purchased a used dirt bike and was trail riding from his house.

Chip and I grew up riding motocross bikes on our 63 acres back in Putnam, Connecticut, but we stopped riding when we went to college. It was the first time I had ridden a dirt bike in 18 years. I had forgotten how much I loved it! Not only was riding a dirt bike an adrenaline high, but it also gave my mind a break from continually worrying about the gym.

Within a month, I purchased a used Yamaha YZ125 and started riding with a couple of gym members in the local sandpits. What began with a simple ride behind my brother's house in Maine turned into a real commitment to motocross racing and culminated in my winning the 40+ Novice New England Motocross Championship. I was finally learning how to live a more balanced and Authentic Life. I learned how to balance work and play.

My days consisted of going to work around 9:00 a.m. and

completing my tasks by noon, grabbing lunch with Elliot if he was around, then heading to the practice track in my Planet Fitness lettered van, loaded with my dirt bike and gear. With everyone else working at their nine-to-five, I had the track to myself with two or three other riders. When the "after work" crowd came streaming into the pits around 5:00 p.m., I was already on my way home for dinner.

I met Mike Treadwell one day at my gym. Mike is one of a handful of local New England motocross legends. Mike lived in Enfield and walked into my gym with his shoulder in a sling. Tread had recently had reconstructive shoulder surgery after a racing accident. He asked if I could help him with his recovery, so I became his personal trainer. I helped Tread rehab his shoulder and get in the best riding shape of his life; he helped me get better at racing a dirt bike.

My friendship with Tread led to becoming friends with John Dowd, Keith Johnson, Tony Lorusso, and other New England motocross legends. I even rode at Doug Henry's private track in Torrington. When the Professional Motocross Series raced at nearby Southwick, Massachusetts, many of the top-level pros worked out at my gym.

I was finally living the life I had always dreamed about.

When crashing a dirt bike began taking a toll on my body,

I switched from racing motocross to indoor karts. My afternoons and evenings transitioned from the outdoor MX track to the indoor karting track at On Track Karting in Wallingford, Connecticut. For the next couple of years, I was obsessed with getting the fastest lap time at the facility and competing in the weekly racing leagues.

Much like meeting Mike Treadwell when I was obsessed with racing motocross, I met a young car racer named Ryan Preece and had a blast racing against him in the gas-powered karts. For the 2021 season, Ryan drove the #37 Chevy Camaro ZL1 for JTG Daugherty Racing in the NASCAR Cup Series.

Through hard work and suffering, I had created a life that allowed me to follow my Purpose at work, while giving me the financial stability and free time to pursue the activities I loved outside of work. Owning my business was the catalyst to creating such Freedom. From swimming in the embalming fluid of Corporate America to starting my own consulting company, to purchasing a failing World Gym with every penny I had accumulated—the struggle finally resulted in a daily life that was entirely under my control. Each day I did what I wanted to do with the people I wanted to be with. I couldn't ask for a better life.

My story is one of rebelling against Society's norms and taking the Path less traveled. Success for me hinged on correctly answering the same question at every fork in the road: "What direction will give me more authority to call my own shots?" As a result, I always veered in the direction of creating autonomy. I created a life where I could get my work done by noon (doing something I loved) and spend the rest of my day immersed in the activities I loved.

Even after my family moved to New Hampshire and I sold my ownership interest in Blitz along with my gym in Connecticut, maintaining my Freedom was priority number one. I had a fleeting thought of getting a job in Corporate America again and using the sales proceeds to ensure a secure retirement. But I quickly regained my senses and looked for another franchise opportunity to provide the Freedom I loved. Once you experience the entrepreneurial Freedom I've had, it's almost impossible to get back in Society's Box.

Sola Salon Studios is a franchise that offers the most autonomy I've yet to see from a franchisor. You don't even need any employees if you are good at giving tours and maintaining your books. With the Freedom offered by this new business model, I've had the time to write this book, coach my daughter's sports teams, care for my mother with the early onset of dementia resulting from her TBI, and consult with other entrepreneurs looking to find their Freedom.

Autonomy comes from owning an asset that produces an

income stream to cover your household expenses, fill your retirement savings, and provide enough extra cash flow to indulge in your current passions. The key is having systems in place that give you time to pursue those passions, all with doing a little day-to-day work once the systems are working!

The asset can be a business, real estate investment, or royalties from a successful book. The key is finding the spark that illuminates the futility of chasing Society's goals and opens your eyes to a new reality. My spark was reading *The Adventure of Leadership: An Unorthodox Business Guide* by Hap Klopp, founder of The North Face. That was the "thing" that finally flipped the switch in my mind. After reading that book, I knew I needed to own my own company.

I wrote this book to provide the same spark for you. You picked up this book for a reason. Believe it. You are the type of person who can't work for someone else for the rest of your life. I understand. Completely. I implore you to go Against the Grain and follow the Path that eventually allows you to say what UCONN basketball coach Jim Calhoun so succinctly stated: "I never went to work. I don't have a job. I *coach*." Fill in your blank. Find your *why* and write it in. Then find a way to make it your business. I assure you, your life will never be the same!

This sentiment doesn't just come from one coach or one

successful person. One example I love is Evan Hafer, the CEO of Black Rifle Coffee. Evan was a former Green Beret who later worked for the CIA and got burnt out working for the government. He wanted to know he could survive and feed himself outside of the government. Evan always had a passion for brewing a perfect cup of coffee. The story of Black Rifle Coffee embodies what it takes to turn a passion into a successful business while surrounding yourself with people you genuinely love. He knows the truth of what it takes to live beneath your means and keep focused on your Purpose when all you want to do is throw in the towel.

On the *Order of Man* podcast, Evan clearly explains to Ryan Michler that he started Black Rifle Coffee because he wanted his Freedom. In his own words, "I needed to own my own company so I could own my own life. If you love what you do, and you love your family, you *win*. You get twenty-four hours a day of doing what you love." *That's the real definition of success.* My thesis on living an Authentic Life hinges on finding a business that supports your Purpose and connects with you so strongly on an emotional level that you get goose bumps thinking about it. Autonomy is the goal—the Freedom to drive in the opposite direction of traffic every day.

The Freedom to wake up each morning and make the decision to spend four hours getting work done at your business, then heading out to the practice track with your dirt bike to get ready for the weekend's race.

The Freedom to meet your spouse at 3:00 p.m. at your favorite bar to kick off happy hour.

The Freedom to volunteer as a chaperone for as many of your kid's school trips as you can.

The Freedom to help a parent suffering from a debilitating disease later in life.

I don't know of a better way to accomplish this in your life than owning your own business. Only your family, your friends, and your employees have any say regarding your daily decisions.

But there is a dark side to entrepreneurial success.

I know many successful entrepreneurs who have *less* Freedom than employees with a nine-to-five. Some let their businesses grow too large and never put in the systems to empower their employees to handle the daily decision-making. In others, the business owners continue to be driven by Society's lies of wealth, power, and status, and they continue to have an insatiable desire for *more*. The result, even as an owner, is little to no daily Freedom.

It is counterintuitive, but you find Freedom by knowing when to say no to many of the opportunities that present themselves. Determine what Freedom truly means to you, what that daily life looks like, and stay true to it. Once you've set the bar for the level of autonomy you want in your life, please don't keep trying to move it higher.

Know when to say, "Enough"!

CONCLUSION

YOU HAVE TO JUMP INTO THE
DEEP END OF THE POOL

"Life is either a daring adventure or nothing."

— HELEN KELLER

My daughter stood on the edge of the hotel's indoor swimming pool. She had slowly inched her way down the coping to the deep end of the pool. Brenna had her rainbow-colored swim goggles on and was gently rocking back and forth, looking down into the water. My wife could hear Brenna say something to herself and asked, "What are you saying?"

Brenna looked up at Stephanie through her fog-filled goggles and said, "Come on, Brenna, don't be such a pussy." My wife gasped as my daughter looked back down at the water and jumped! There is simply no better way to conclude this book than saying what needs to be said. *You can't be a pussy if you hope to live an Authentic Life.*

After my wife labeled me Father of the Year, I apologized to Brenna (while laughing inside) and explained that "pussy" wasn't a word she should speak in public. But deep within my soul, I knew I was doing my job as her father. I imagined what her life might become had we never taught her the value of taking calculated risks. Brenna had been overcome by her fear of swimming, sitting in a chair by the side of the pool, watching her friends have a blast. Her confidence eroded at such a young age and impacted other areas of her life. I was ecstatic. Brenna had jumped all on her own.

It happens to us as adults. We get trapped in Society's Box because the risk of change seems too great, so we miss out on all the fun that comes with living an Authentic Life. Please, don't let this happen to you. If you find yourself standing on the edge of the pool and cannot jump, I challenge you to look at this obstacle from a different perspective. Instead of viewing the act of jumping as the difficult part of the problem, ask yourself this question: "What's the risk of staying on the safe Path and never finding my Freedom?"

What's the risk of staying in a job you aren't even interested in because the pay is good and you fit in with everyone else? Of working long hours and spending massive amounts of time away from your family so you can finally get the words "vice president" printed on your business card? Of spending way too much money on a house trying to impress people you don't even know?

The risk is waking up 30 years in the future and realizing the only thing that brought any fulfillment to your life was getting your golf handicap into the single digits! It's the knowledge that if you keep your head down and do what the guy in the corner office tells you, your reward will be a shiny new pair of "golden handcuffs" getting slapped on your wrists as you near your retirement! Have you ever asked yourself why Corporate America uses handcuffs to keep their best performers on the payroll as they near retirement? Aren't handcuffs used to keep people in prison?

Life is short. Living your life with authenticity and finding the Freedom to do the things you are passionate about is always worth the risk. Everyone dreams about living such a life. Everyone says they are working on their plan to get there. But most never jump into the deep end of the pool.

Instead, they fall in line with the rest of the herd, addicted to the comfort of Society's Path, pointing to the size of their annual salary and the weeks of vacation they have earned as justification for believing the lies.

I know. I started down that Path.

I was addicted to Society's lies during my climb up the corporate ladder. I loved what I was doing. I was obsessed with changing the culture within that old unionized plant, but the job ended up owning my life. I ignored girlfriends, family, and friends on my climb. I even ignored my health. I was obsessed with becoming the plant manager so I could run things my way. But there is no such thing as "running things my way" within Corporate America's walls. It did feel good getting promoted regularly and having the extra money to purchase nicer cars and a new house on the right side of town. From Society's point of view, everything was going my way.

But the farther down Society's Path I traveled, the more disillusioned I became. I realized early in my career that my Vision of success had very little in common with Society's view. Most people never see the shackles Society has clamped on their ankles. Going Against the Grain requires you to break the shackles any way you can. The earlier in life, the better. The longer you wait, the stronger the chains become. Please take my word for it. You will never feel ready to follow your own Path. You just have to jump into the deep end of the pool and trust the fact that if you're following your Purpose and are willing to put work before pleasure, you will eventually find your Freedom. But first, let's crush the most common excuse people have for staying in Society's Box:

"I don't have the time."

A "normal" person's week, stuck in Society's Box, looks something like this:

Total available hours in a week:
7 days × 24 hours = 168 hours per week (for everyone)

Typical workweek (Monday through Friday) = 120 hours			
Sleep:	8 hours × 5 days	=	40 hours per workweek (33%)
Breakfast and get ready for work:	1 hour × 5 days	=	5 hours per workweek (4%)
Commute to and from work:	1 hour × 5 days	=	5 hours per week (4%)
Work and lunch:	9 hours × 5 days	=	45 hours per week (38%)
Dinner:	1 hour × 5 days	=	5 hours per week (4%)
Total used time per week		**=**	**100 hours (83%)**
Remaining personal time = 20 hours per workweek or 4 hours per weekday			
Typical weekend (Saturday and Sunday) = 48 hours			
Sleep:	8 hours × 2 days	=	16 hours per weekend (33%)
Breakfast:	1 hour × 2 days	=	2 hours per weekend (4%)
Lunch:	1 hour × 2 days	=	2 hours per weekend (4%)
Dinner (at restaurant):	3 hours × 2 days	=	6 hours per weekend (12%)
Total used time per weekend		**=**	**26 hours (54%)**
Remaining personal time = 48 − 26 = 22 hours per weekend or 11 hours per weekend day (45%)			

Total personal time = 20 + 22 = 44 hours per week

Most of us have somewhere close to 40 hours per week to commit to making a significant change in our lives! *Not having enough time is never an acceptable excuse for not living an Authentic Life.*

Start the task of building your three-legged stool. Without it, you'll never reach the key to unlock the door that leads to your Authentic Life. Leg 1 is your Vision of Freedom. You need to have a clear Vision of what Freedom means to you; it's the foundation upon which you will build your new life. Leg 2 is your Purpose. Think long and hard about what gives you goose bumps in life. Develop your Why Statement and uncover your Purpose. Finally, Leg 3 is the people your Purpose will serve. Understand if your Purpose doesn't hinge on helping others succeed, you don't have a Purpose. Instead, you have a goal, and there's a hell of a big difference between the two.

When your goal centers on getting everything *you* want in life, you may reach it, but end up empty in the process. Understand that bigger and nicer homes, more expensive vehicles, and the increased social status obtained as you climb the corporate ladder don't result in more Freedom; they strengthen the chains that keep you a prisoner within Society's Box. Such desires stem from ego, and ego is the enemy of Freedom. As David Brooks so perfectly states in his book *The Second Mountain*, Freedom and Purpose come from community and passion, not self-identity and ego.

Step up on your stool and find the key hidden above your unique door. Finally, you are ready to start on the Path called Against the Grain. It's time to face your fears. By its very nature, taking the Path called Against the Grain puts you face-to-face with fear. Fear of judgment from those still on Society's Path, fear of failure, and even fear of success.

I am sure of one thing. You'll never take the first and most difficult step on the Path called Against the Grain until you realize that fear is just another form of excitement. You're feeling the same butterflies in your stomach that you always felt when it was time to play your soccer game or ask that boy or girl in your class to go on a date. You're not scared; you're excited!

You've established a monthly budget, and you're tracking your weekly spending. You've reduced any fixed expenses to a minimum and cut way back on discretionary spending. You understand the most fundamental rule of all: *if you spend more than you make, you'll never find Freedom.*

Freedom comes from keeping things small and simple. Constantly striving for more keeps you chained in Society's Box. "Enough" is the word that will help set you free. You are starting small and focusing on opening the best business you can, making it perform as well as it possibly can before considering doing more. You've told the people closest to you of your decision to follow your authentic Path. You are no longer in bondage to the opinions of others. You're deaf to the nay-sayers, those too afraid to leap into the deep end of the pool. You understand your circle of friends will shrink down to the handful of people that genuinely support you.

Your Path will be incredibly difficult and require a tremendous amount of work. Going Against the Grain requires the discipline to ignore the comforts of life and do the work necessary to follow your Purpose. You've built the confidence to know you are capable of persevering when times get tough. You've filled your cookie jar to the brim.

You understand that Freedom comes from owning a business and creating a community of like-minded people who believe in your Purpose. When you focus on improving your customers' lives and your employees' lives, your life improves drastically. Your Freedom comes from having employees that embrace your Vision and treat your business like their own. You embrace the concept of servant leadership and the belief that "It's all about them."

You understand that once you decide to jump into the deep end of the pool, the only short-term goal is to feed your business until it can feed you back. That business can range from writing a book, starting a podcast, opening a gym, purchasing a franchise, or hanging out your shingle as a consultant. In the beginning, you will be grossly underpaid. But if you refuse to give up and commit to putting in the work, you'll enjoy a life filled with personal Freedom and the autonomy to live each day according to your plan, and no one else's.

Think hard about what your life will look like five to 10 years down the road. You can stay on the comfortable

Path, live a lackluster life, and never put in the hard work required to figure out who you are.

Or...

You can start a business you are obsessed with and enjoy the process of getting a little bit better at serving your customers day after day. Your goal isn't to become a multimillionaire next year; you are happy living within your means and doing things that bring joy to your life. Financial success will come over time by doing the little things correctly, day after day, year after year. Your goal is the autonomy you'll create with outstanding employees and excellent operating systems.

This combination will give you the flexibility to spend more time with your family while creating a tight circle of like-minded friends outside of work who share the same passions you have.

Stop imagining this life. Say yes to being you and living an Authentic Life!

Break out of Society's Box. Just because your parents, your teachers, and most of your friends told you it was necessary to go to college and climb the corporate ladder doesn't mean you need to stay stuck in an unfulfilling career for the rest of your life. The life most of us strive to obtain isn't that great of a life. When we were young and full of wonder and hope, did we truly believe that success in life would look anything like this?

> Wake up. Eat a quick breakfast. Drive to work in nine-to-five traffic. Work hard building someone else's business, performing a job that provides little personal fulfillment. Drive home in nine-to-five traffic. Eat dinner and watch TV until you fall asleep. Count down the days until Friday. Repeat for 40 years. Retire and hope to enjoy the last 15 years of your life.

I wrote this book to provide the inspiration and the plan to help you jump into the deep end of the pool. So put on your goggles, hold your nose, and *jump!* Please remember, there is no such thing as "instant" success. Many begin on the Path to living an Authentic Life, but few have the heart and persistence to finish what they start.

The key personal traits needed to summit the Path called Against the Grain are a high level of self-confidence and a willingness to endure. Promise yourself you'll never give up, and I promise you'll experience the Freedom of always driving in the opposite direction of nine-to-five traffic. You'll create the autonomy to work 10 to 20 hours per week on a business you love, and to spend the rest of your time mastering the current activity you are passionate about. That's a life worth living.

Go live *your* life. Figure out what truly drives you, and

figure out how to help others experience your gift, whatever that may be. And remember the most important lesson in this book:

The function of Freedom is to free someone else!

ACKNOWLEDGMENTS

Writing a book has been my goal ever since I read *The Adventure of Leadership: An Unorthodox Business Guide* by Hap Klopp, founder of The North Face, over 25 years ago. Hap opened my eyes to a new reality, that of the iconoclast. The person who lives life on their terms and no one else's. That book provided the final bit of motivation I needed to break out of Society's Box and leave Corporate America's confines. I hope that *Against the Grain* provides the same inspiration for you to break free of others' expectations and follow your authentic Path in life.

The process of completing this book has been one of the most challenging endeavors I have ever volunteered for in my life. I would have never accomplished this lofty goal without guidance and support from the outstanding team at Scribe Media. I am forever indebted to Tucker Max, Hal Clifford,

Emily Gindlesparger, Neddie Ann Underwood, Hussein Al-Baiaty, Mckenna Bailey, Erik van Mechelen, Katherine Shady, Erin Michelle Sky, Natalia A. Pagán Serrano, Geneva Ross, Elizabeth Oliver, Laura Cail, Paulina Sliwa, and Esty Pittman. I also need to thank my October 2019 Scribe Guided Author cohort I met personally in Austin, Texas. The resulting Scribe Fam Group we created on WhatsApp provided a never-ending source of motivation and accountability to stick to the task at hand and finish this book.

Even with Scribe's professional guidance, this book would have never made it to print without the patience and undying support from my wife, Stephanie, and our beautiful daughter, Brenna. They never gave me any grief when I declined a fun afternoon hike to stay home to work on the book. They endured the read-aloud portion of the editing process and provided invaluable feedback that made this book better.

Without growing up in the dysfunctional family unit consisting of my father, Charles S. Perkins, mother, Vivian E. Perkins, and older brother, Charles R. (Chip) Perkins, I wouldn't have a story to tell. So much of our upbringing was wrong, yet my brother and I learned the value of hard work and eventually found our paths to success. I will always love each of you with all of my heart.

I am forever grateful to my grandfather and stepgrandmother, Louis and Bertha Defilippo, for being living examples of the simplicity of happiness. I learned how to live life correctly through your actions and advice. I can't wait to see you both again when the time is right.

Special thanks to my high school football coach, Robert Deveau, for showing me what effective leadership is and for hardwiring the value of teamwork into my psyche. The same thanks to my high school physics teacher, Dr. Louise Pempek, for being a living example of the joy that comes to those who spend their life doing something they love.

A heartfelt thanks to Donald Aube, Barry Bayly, Henry Fijalkowski, and Edward Petrovitz from the Torrington Company for helping me prove that managers and workers can thrive by working together and seeing themselves as equals.

Thanks to Michael Grondahl, Marc Grondahl, and Chris Rondeau for your many years of friendship and for providing the Planet Fitness franchising opportunity to many. Thanks to Mark Spengler, my business partner at Blitz Indoor Trampoline Park, for being such a great student of the game of business.

My work life would be empty if it weren't for all the managers who have worked alongside me in my different businesses. Seeing each of you rise to the many challenges life always brings has never stopped giving me goose bumps. Thank you for believing in me, Danah Cordeira, Lori Sneitka, Sarah Caron, Laurie Letourneau, James Pettinato, Samuel Robbins, Matt Schnepp, Nicole Lazzari, and Willie Brown.

And finally, to that core group of friends who have been by my side through all of life's obstacles, my wolf pack, and those I would gladly die for. I can never fully explain how much you guys mean to me. Steve Chenail, Michael Tremose, Anthony Montuori, Scott Haeffner, Wally Crumb, Nelson Minier, and Elliot Wilson—I love each of you with every ounce of my heart.

APPENDIX

ADDITIONAL RESOURCES

I've organized the following resources by chapter. These resources helped guide me throughout my journey *Against the Grain*! Utilize them in your effort to find your authentic voice and create the life you've been dreaming about.

CHAPTER 1

ARTICLES

- "Taming the Mammoth" by Tim Urban, www.waitbut why.com

POEMS

- "The Man in the Glass" by Anonymous

PODCASTS

- *Hands and Daylight*, #32: "In Bondage to Fear and the Opinion of Others"

WEBSITES

- Understand Myself: The Big Five Aspects Scale, www.understandmyself.com

CHAPTER 2
BOOKS

- *Discipline Equals Freedom: Field Manual* by Jocko Willink
- *75 Hard* by Andy Frisella

CHAPTER 3
ARTICLES

- "My 10 Commandments of Freedom" by James Altucher, www.jamesaltucher.com

CHAPTER 4
BOOKS

- *Find Your Why* by Simon Sinek
- *Shoe Dog* by Phil Knight
- *The War of Art* by Steven Pressfield

PODCASTS

- *The 3-of-7 Podcast*, #6: "Jesse Itzler Lessons Learned in Life and Ultra Running"

CHAPTER 5

BOOKS

- *Ego Is the Enemy* by Ryan Holiday

CHAPTER 6

SONGS

- "Fear Is a Liar" by Zach Williams

BOOKS

- *Fearvana* by Akshay Nanavati
- *Mastering Fear* by Brandon Webb

CHAPTER 7

PODCASTS

- *Hands and Daylight*, #40, "Barefoot and Pregnant"
- *The James Altucher Show*, #318, "Scary, but Not Impossible...Leaving the Job You Hate for the One You'd Love"

CHAPTER 8

VIDEOS

- *The Simplicity of Happiness*, Erwin Darmali, www. youtube.com

BOOKS

- *Stillness Is the Key* by Ryan Holiday

CHAPTER 9
BOOKS

- *Can't Hurt Me* by David Goggins

CHAPTER 10
BOOKS

- *The Adventure of Leadership: An Unorthodox Business Guide* by Hap Klopp

PODCASTS

- *Order of Man*, #186, "Purpose, Passion, and Profit with Evan Hafer of Black Rifle Coffee"

CONCLUSION
BOOKS

- *The Second Mountain* by David Brooks

ABOUT THE AUTHOR

CRAIG PERKINS is a husband, father, and accomplished business leader with expertise as a senior-level manager in a Fortune 500 company and long-time private business owner. He grew up following Society's rules: get good grades in high school, go to college, get a degree in a field with high salary potential, land a job with a Fortune 500 company, and enjoy the social status and prestige that comes with climbing the corporate ladder.

Craig gave it all up to follow a Path he calls Against the Grain. A course whose destination is personal autonomy and the Freedom to drive in the opposite direction of nine-to-five traffic. This book details his struggle to live life authentically. A life created by owning a business that furthered his Purpose and gave him the time to pursue activities he was passionate about alongside the people who mattered most in his life. Craig uses his experience to help others kick down the walls of Society's Box and create lives filled with autonomy.

Learn more at www.craigaperkins.com.

CPSIA information can be obtained
at www.ICGtesting.com
Printed in the USA
LVHW030318030222
709976LV00004B/125

9 781544 525419